INSTANT BARGAINS

600+

Ways to Shrink Your Grocery Bills and Eat Well for Less

KIMBERLY DANGER

 sourcebooks

Published by Sourcebooks, Inc.
P.O. Box 4410, Naperville, Illinois 60567-4410
(630) 961-3900
Fax: (630) 961-2168
www.sourcebooks.com

Library of Congress Cataloging-in-Publication Data

Danger, Kimberly.
 Instant bargains : 600+ ways to shrink your grocery bills and eat well for less / by Kimberly Danger.
     p. cm.
 1. Grocery shopping--United States. 2. Low budget cookery. 3. Consumer education--United States. I. Title.
 TX356.D36 2010
 641.3'1--dc22
                        2009030723

Printed and bound in the United States of America.
VP 10 9 8 7 6 5 4 3 2 1

To my parents

CONTENTS

ACKNOWLEDGMENTS

This book would have never taken shape if it had not been for some very special people.

First and foremost, thanks to all the Mommysavers members who contributed their tips and stories. This book, as well as the success of Mommysavers.com, wouldn't be possible without you.

Thanks to my wonderful family and friends for their encouragement and support. To my parents, Bob and Jean Vajgrt, for teaching me ways to eat well for less so I could share them with others. To Scott for being the wonderful and supportive husband that he is, and my kids, Sydney and Nicholas, for bearing with me as I spent months writing and testing out new and unusual foods. Thanks to my friends for cheering me on and helping me out with child care so I had uninterrupted time to write.

I'm also extremely grateful for those who support me professionally, including the terrific editors at Sourcebooks, Shana Drehs and Sara Appino. Your tips helped me create an even better final product. Thanks to the staff at Trone and Uniroyal for giving me a forum in which to spread my frugal message. Thanks as well to The Kotchen Group for getting me out in the public eye.

INTRODUCTION

The U.S. Department of Labor estimates that the average American family of four spends $8,513 per year on groceries. That translates to over $700 per month. With a busy family and two kids of my own, I know how hard it can be to feed a family healthy food on a budget. While grocery bills often consume the biggest part of your paycheck after housing and auto, the grocery bill is also one of the easiest areas to cut back on. That's what led me to write this book.

As founder and creator of Mommysavers.com, I've read about hundreds of ways that families in our online community are saving on groceries and eating out. Everyone has a different approach, which is why this book includes a wide array of tips, each of which is set off by a $. Unlike some other books you might find, *Instant Bargains* is not a programmatic lifestyle that requires lots of time and energy in order to reap the benefits. Rather, this book is designed to give you information you can use right away, today, to save money on your food bills. Even if you don't live near a store that doubles coupons, have the space to stockpile, or have tons of time to comparison-shop, you'll learn how to find some great grocery bargains. The key is finding the methods that are the best fit with your own lifestyle.

Getting the best value for your money can be tricky when it comes to food. There's much more to consider than just the price of the ingredients. You also have to look at nutritional value, prep time, and other variables. It isn't always about buying cheaper; it's about buying *smarter.*

Eating is also a social experience, a time to share with family and friends. It should be an enjoyable and memorable experience. It's just as much about breaking bread with loved ones and forging bonds as it is about nourishing our bodies. If you're only focusing on getting the cheapest products you can, you're missing out on the other parts of the equation.

While I wish there were a magic wand I could wave to make gourmet meals magically appear on my table every night, I have yet to figure that out. There are, however, many different strategies that can help any family reduce its food budget without sacrificing quality. Inside this book you'll discover tried-and-true methods as well as some exciting new ways to save made possible by technology in recent years. How much you save depends on how many of the strategies you can take on.

With a little planning and creativity, you can accomplish great things in the kitchen on even the most limited budget and enjoy some quality food and family time as well.

Happy saving!

—Kimberly Danger

GET ORGANIZED TO SAVE

Organization is the key to saving money in many areas of your budget, and this is especially true in the kitchen. Before you set foot in the grocery store, it pays to have a plan. A weekly menu and grocery list are a great place to start.

Menu Planning

Organized and efficient shopping starts with a menu plan. Don't let a lack of time get in the way of sitting down to write out a plan. Once you get organized, it takes just a few minutes and ends up saving you loads of time (and money) in the long run. Additionally, you'll be able to offer meals with better nutritional value to your family.

You'll see that many of these general shopping tips will be expanded upon later in the book—we'll just start with the big picture and work our way toward the details.

START SIMPLY SO YOU WON'T BE INTIMIDATED BY THE PROCESS.
If compiling an entire week's worth of menus seems like too

daunting a task, aim for three or four. You'll be inspired by your success and want to build on it.

FIRST, DECIDE HOW OFTEN YOU WANT TO VISIT THE GROCERY STORE. A weekly menu plan works well for most families because you will always have fresh produce and you'll be able to take advantage of weekly grocery store sales. (Refer to the **weekly menu planning worksheet** on page 6.) By making only one trip to the store each week, you're saving time and gas, but an even bigger benefit is that you'll be avoiding impulse purchases, which, according to sociologist Paco Underhill, can account for two-thirds of all purchases. As you become more adept at organizing things, you may want to try a biweekly or even a monthly plan.

GRAB YOUR CALENDAR. Decide how many meals you'll be responsible for in the time between visits to the grocery store. Which days will you eat breakfast and lunch at home as well as dinner? Will there be nights when you won't be at home, or times when you'll have more people to feed than your immediate family? Take time constraints into consideration when planning meals. Having a slow-cooker meal on a busy night makes sense if you don't have time to cook.

TAKE AN INVENTORY OF WHAT YOU HAVE. Take special note of any perishables nearing their expiration dates. Incorporate them as much as possible when planning meals to avoid wasting food. This is also a great time to clean out your refrigerator.

Toss anything that is no longer fresh, and give the shelves a quick wipe-down.

STOCK UP ON STAPLES. If you're running low on things like sugar, salt, flour, eggs, and milk, make sure you add them to your list.

BE SPECIFIC IN WRITING YOUR LIST. Using general terms such as "pasta" or "cheese" leaves a lot of room for interpretation. How many boxes of pasta do you need, and what size? What kinds and varieties of cheeses? Sometimes even planned purchases can get out of control. When you create your list, be as specific as possible.

NEXT, SEE WHAT'S ON SALE AT THE GROCERY STORE. Search for recipes that combine what you have on hand at home with the best deals at your grocery store. For example, if you have potatoes and carrots on hand and beef roast is on sale this week, add a pot roast to your menu plan.

PLAN YOUR PROTEIN. Since this is likely the most expensive part of your meal, plan it first. Keep in mind that you don't have to serve a big slab of meat with each meal. Consider main courses such as stir-fries or one-pot meals that use meat as part of the dish but not the main focus. Or consider using beans as a meat extender or in a casserole.

"I'm a firm believer that menu planning saves both time and money. Before the start of each month, I get out my index box of recipes and plan our meals for the next four weeks. I start with a blank calendar and start plugging in the food. To ensure variety, I plan a different type of meal for each day. Sunday is Crock-Pot or sandwich day, Monday is chicken, Tuesday is breakfast for dinner or Italian, Wednesday is Mexican, Thursday is beef, Friday is fish or pizza, and Saturday is an easy, on-the-go meal."

—SONJA GOODCHILD, EAST TROY, WISCONSIN

INCLUDE FRUGAL MEALS EACH WEEK. Good ideas are a planned leftovers meal, a time-crunch meal (one that's premade and stored in the freezer or a slow-cooker meal), a meatless meal, a soup-and-sandwich night, and a breakfast-for-dinner night of pancakes, waffles, or even cold cereal. Use the menu planning worksheet on page 6 as a guide.

AVOID WASTE. When perishable food is on your list, plan multiple ways to use it up. If you're going to be buying a bag of celery for one recipe, how can you incorporate it into others on your menu plan?

INCORPORATE VARIETY. Does your menu plan include a variety of foods such as pasta, rice, beans, fish, poultry, and red meat as well as fruits and vegetables? Does it include a variety of textures and flavors? If it doesn't, chances are you'll get bored with what you have on hand and be tempted to return to the store for something else.

🪙 **EXPAND YOUR RECIPE COLLECTION.** Avoid eating the same meal more than once or twice per month. Build up your recipe collection to include at least fifty family-friendly meals that include a wide array of main dishes, sides, and healthy desserts to avoid frugal fatigue.

🪙 **DON'T FORGET THE SNACKS.** Meals take the most planning, but you'll also want to include some healthy snacks on your shopping list too.

🪙 **BEFORE GOING TO THE STORE, COMPUTE THE COST OF EACH MEAL.** Computing the cost of homemade meals can be a huge eye-opener. Sometimes more expensive cuts of fresh fish and meat, when paired with a simple vegetable, cost the same as—or even less than—prepackaged frozen meals or casseroles with a lot of thrifty ingredients. Additionally, simple meals like this usually involve much less prep time and fewer wasted ingredients. Being aware of the cost can help you make well-informed buying decisions. Compare the casserole meal here with the fresh fish meal on page 8.

CASSEROLE MEAL (CHEESY CHICKEN AND RICE)

1 10.5-ounce can cream of chicken soup	$1.69
¾ cup long-grain rice (cost based on 1-pound bag of rice)	$1.79
1 12-ounce bag frozen broccoli (store brand)	$1.39
Boneless, skinless chicken breasts (1 pound)	$3.19
1 cup cheddar cheese (cost based on 2-cup bag)	$2.29
Total:	$10.35

Create a worksheet of your own or feel free to reproduce this one for your own use.

Weekly Menu Planning Worksheet

MEAT MAINSTAY

PLANNED LEFTOVER MEAL

BREAKFAST FOR DINNER

TIME-CRUNCH MEAL

SOUP-AND-SANDWICH NIGHT OR MEATLESS MEAL

MEAL 5

JUST-FOR-FUN NIGHT

MEAL 6

CLEAN-OUT-THE-REFRIGERATOR NIGHT

MEAL 7

HEALTHY SNACKS

BREAKFASTS AND LUNCHES

FRESH FISH AND VEGGIE MEAL (TILAPIA AND BROCCOLI)

Fresh tilapia (1 pound)	$5.89
1 16-ounce bag frozen broccoli (store brand)	$1.39
Total:	$7.28

SUBSTITUTE ITEMS IF NECESSARY. Be prepared to make smart substitutions when you get to the store. If ground beef is on sale and it's a good substitute for more expensive ground turkey, make the trade. It's fine to sway from your list as long as what you're doing makes financial sense.

PERHAPS MOST IMPORTANTLY, BE FLEXIBLE. You may find that something you planned on buying isn't available or just doesn't look good. By improvising and adjusting your meal plan accordingly, you can save even more money.

WATCH OUT!

Having a list can backfire. When people shop with a list, they tend to "reward" themselves with impulse buys when they're done shopping, says Dr. Brian Wansink, author of *Mindless Eating*.

MENU PLANNING WEBSITES AND SOFTWARE

If sitting down and creating a meal plan sounds like a daunting task, consider some tools to make it simple. New technologies have made it easier than ever to make getting organized in the kitchen a fun process.

GROCERY STORE WEBSITES. These have come a long way in recent years. Many offer great resources such as recipes, printable coupons, and online shopping capabilities. Some grocery stores have menu planning features on their websites, some of which work for any shopper regardless of whether you have that store in your area. For example, it doesn't matter if Jewel is the only store in your area, because you can use Harristeeter.com to plan your list even if you aren't shopping there. Among the store websites:

- Aldi.com
- Rainbowfoods.com
- Harristeeter.com
- Kroger.com
- Winndixiegrocerystores.com
- Wegmans.com

BIGOVEN.COM. This subscription-based website allows you to upload and organize your recipes, print grocery lists, create meal plans, import photos, calculate nutritional information, create custom cookbooks, and interact with other Big Oven members. It's free to join; premium memberships are by subscription only. Premium members can upload shopping lists directly to their PDAs or SmartPhones.

Bottom line: Great for tech geeks.

ALLRECIPES.COM. Allrecipes boasts a huge readership as well as an expansive recipe collection. Its advanced search option makes it easy to find recipes based on the ingredients you already have at home, which can help you save loads of money. Its free membership includes photo uploading, recipe storage, and printable grocery lists.

Bottom line: Lots of options with free membership.

RECIPEZAAR.COM. Recipezaar.com also provides free memberships, which includes recipe storage and participation in its online forum. With a premium membership subscription, members can create custom menu plans, grocery lists, and custom cookbooks.

Bottom line: Great for those willing to pay for membership.

SCANMYRECIPES.COM. Simply send this company your recipes via prepaid UPS mailer, and it'll scan each of your recipes, transcribe them in plain text, burn them onto a CD-ROM for you, and ship them back. You can also find your recipes stored online on this site's companion website, keyingredient.com, and available for emailing, sharing, and printing custom cookbooks.

Bottom Line: Ideal for anyone who isn't computer-savvy.

OTHER NOTABLE RECIPE SITES:

- Epicurious.com
- Myrecipes.com
- Chowhound.com
- Foodnetwork.com
- Kraft.com
- Tasteofhome.com

Shopping Lists

Keeping a running shopping list can help you avoid being stuck without an essential pantry staple or ingredient for your favorite recipe.

> **CREATE A STANDARD FAMILY SHOPPING LIST** in spreadsheet form and store it on your computer. Print it out and keep a copy on your refrigerator. When you run out of something, simply circle the item on your list. When you're ready to go shopping, you'll know exactly what you need.

> **USE COLUMNS CLASSIFYING EACH ITEM** as "produce," "meat," "frozen foods," "dairy," etc., according to where it is located in the store. This cuts down on backtracking to get something you missed on the first pass. The more time you spend in the store, the more likely you are to buy something that wasn't on your list. This spreadsheet can also be the basis of the price book you create (on page 19).

You can also use some forward-thinking websites and other technology to create a grocery list for you.

> **GROCERY IQ.** GroceryIQ is a grocery shopping application for the iPhone or iPod Touch. The application comes preloaded with more than 130,000 items commonly found in supermarkets across America. The software enables users to organize their personal shopping lists by store, aisle, buying history, and favorites, as well as customizing item sizes. Available for download on iTunes for $0.99.
>
> www.groceryiq.com

JOTT.COM. Jott.com is a voice-to-text service that converts your spoken words into to-do lists with a simple phone call. Once you link your account, you just call Jott, say, "Remember the milk," then speak your to-do. They place the resulting text on your to-do list and will send it to you via email. It's $9.95 per month for up to forty transcribed voice mails.

http://jott.com

LIFEJOT.COM. Allows you to create grocery lists online. Add custom categories such as aisle or department to make shopping even easier, then print them out or access them anywhere you have Internet (such as on your Smartphone). Free to use.

http://lifejot.com

COZI.COM. Cozi is an organizational site for busy families that includes a shopping list feature. Simply add things to your list from any computer, and either print or have your list texted to any cell phone account. Free to use.

www.cozi.com

YOUR PHONE'S NOTEPAD FEATURE. Use it to create a convenient grocery list that you have at your fingertips wherever you bring your mobile phone.

YOUR MP3 PLAYER'S VOICE RECORDER. Use this to record items on your grocery list as you think of them, then play it back at the store.

"Since becoming a runner, I find that the few hours I have to myself at the gym, I am overwhelmed with the thoughts of things I need to do or accomplish. It would be too awkward to carry around a to-do list and pen with me while I'm there, so instead I purchased an MP3 player that came with an audio voice recorder. When I think of the grocery items I need to buy or recipes I want to try, I just make a recording for myself on the MP3 player and jot everything down when I get home."

—CHRISTY KILGORE, OKLAHOMA CITY, OKLAHOMA

Free (or Low-Cost) Recipe Inspiration

Think you need to buy expensive cookbooks and magazines in order to get creative inspiration when it comes to food? Think again. Some of the easiest and best sources are right at your fingertips and are entirely free.

THE LIBRARY. Your local library is a great frugal resource for cookbooks, cooking magazines, and DVD collections of your favorite cooking programs. If you don't see what you like, consider using interlibrary loan to reserve items on your wish list. That way, you can give a cookbook a trial run before you decide to purchase it for your collection.

MAGAZINE SWAP BINS. Many libraries also have these in their entries. It's another great place to pick up free recipes.

"My husband and I like to try new recipes frequently. Although the Internet is a great resource, I like to read through cookbooks, especially ones with pictures of the recipes. Rather than buying books I will only use a handful of times, I borrow from the library. Not only does my library have hundreds of cookbooks, but I can request them from a dozen other nearby libraries through interlibrary loans."

—SUSIE CHADWICK, DRAPER, UTAH

COOKING BLOGS. There are literally thousands of food blogs on the Internet that offer a plethora of ideas, tips, and recipes. Some are devoted exclusively to cooking on a budget. Find your favorites by entering search strings such as "saving money cooking blogs" or "frugal cooking blogs."

- http://grocerycartchallenge.blogspot.com
- www.leftoverqueen.com
- www.poorgirleatswell.com
- http://thepioneerwoman.com/cooking
- www.5dollardinners.com

USED COOKBOOKS. There's nothing wrong with used cookbooks. In fact, they often have more character than new ones and cost much less. The spills on favorite pages and notes written in the margins all add to their appeal. Thrift stores, rummage sales, and sites like eBay are terrific sources for cookbooks on the cheap. When you're online, use search terms like "gently used" cookbooks.

CHURCH COOKBOOKS. Church group cookbooks in the spiral bindings are especially good for the frugal cook because they're filled with really down-to-earth, simple recipes with ingredients that most people have on hand in their homes. Most contributors put their best foot forward when submitting recipes and only include the ones they've had rave reviews for.

CLASSIC COOKBOOKS. Be on the lookout for classic cookbooks to add to your collection. *The Joy of Cooking, Betty Crocker, Better Homes and Gardens*, and encyclopedia-type cookbooks are great to have among your collection as a resource.

DEPRESSION-ERA COOKBOOKS. Old cookbooks, especially Depression-era cookbooks published in the '30s and early '40s, are great resources for frugal cooks. Since most convenience foods didn't exist back then, you can be assured that almost all the ingredients used are frugal basics. Authentic Depression-era cookbooks can be found in antiques stores, on eBay, and in some thrift stores. Collections of 1930s recipes, such as *Depression Era Recipes* by Patricia Wagner, are still being published as cookbooks today and can be found in major bookstores and online.

THE GOOD OLD DAYS An added benefit to purchasing vintage cookbooks is portion and calorie control. A recent study published in the *Annals of Internal Medicine* shows that over the past seventy years, not only have portion sizes increased in classic cookbooks such as *The Joy of Cooking,* but also the average calorie count per serving has increased by 63 percent!

ONLINE COOKBOOK SAVINGS. Never pay full price for a cookbook. If there's one topping your wish list, try to find it at a discount instead of paying full price. Here are some places to look while you're online:

- Amazon.com Marketplace
- Half.com
- bookcloseouts.com
- booksamillion.com
- eBay.com

(COOKING) BOOK CLUB. If you can't get enough of new cookbooks, consider joining a book club. Most offer new members several books for free or at a reduced price when they join with a requirement to purchase more books before dropping your membership. You can make this work in your favor if you calculate the costs of the additional books before you sign up, as well as take shipping costs into account. Be sure to select the most expensive books on your wish list as the free/reduced-price books, and purchase the cheaper ones to fulfill your commitment.

- Quality Paperback Book Club: www.qpb.com
- The Good Cook: www.thegoodcook.com
- Other places to search for discount books: warehouse stores, discount department stores like T.J. Maxx/ Marshalls, and bookstores at outlet malls

---

INVEST IN A QUALITY COOKBOOK THAT COVERS THE BASICS

When you want to spend money on a cookbook, where should you turn? No kitchen should be without one of the basic cookbooks that gives you step-by-step instructions on the most basic cooking methods. The best ones include

- *The Joy of Cooking*
- *Fannie Farmer Cookbook*
- *More-With-Less Cookbook*
- *New Cook Book by Better Homes and Gardens*

Custom Cookbooks

Once you've amassed a collection of frugal recipes that your family enjoys, having them in a format that allows easy access can help facilitate meal planning even more. Creating your own custom cookbook will put your recipes at your fingertips, making it easier than ever to peruse the contents when you're at a loss for meals to make.

WEB COOKBOOK. Some of the menu planning websites mentioned on page 10 allow you to create your very own custom cookbooks.

Here are some more cookbook printing sites:

- $ Tastebook.com
- $ Lulu.com
- $ Blurb.com
- $ Heritagecookbook.com

$ **A FRUGAL ALTERNATIVE.** Don't have the time to type out all of your recipes or the money to create a custom-bound book? Here's a frugal alternative. Take the contents of your recipe file—magazine clippings, recipe cards, Internet printouts, and all—and simply photocopy them. Handwritten recipes enhance the book, especially if they remind you of a special friend or relative. Insert the pages in plastic sheet protectors to guard from spills and assemble them all in a three-ring binder. The entire project costs less than $10, and it's easy to make multiple copies at the same time to give to friends and family as gifts.

Price Books

A price book is a valuable tool for any shopper, but it's especially handy if you want to stock up on groceries when prices cycle downward, a strategy known as stockpiling. Basically, you use a price book to keep close tabs on prices in various stores over a period of time so that you can spot true bargains. It can also tell you which stores have the lowest everyday prices on the things you buy most often. Armed with this information, you'll be able to spot a great deal when you see it—and you'll know where to shop!

Product	Aisle	Whole Foods	Cub Foods	Aldi	Walmart
Baking powder	Baking	$1.49	$1.97	—	$0.98
Baking soda	Baking	$0.99	$0.69	$0.43	$0.36
Basil, dried, 16 g	Baking	$2.99	—	—	—
Cinnamon, ground, 1.9 oz	Baking	$2.99	—	—	—
Sugar, confectioners', 24 oz	Baking	$3.99	$1.65	—	$1.44
Cornstarch, 16 oz	Baking	$1.79	$1.43	—	—
Cornmeal, 24 oz	Baking	$2.99	$1.86	—	—
Cumin, 45 g	Baking	$2.99	—	—	—
Dill, 4 g	Baking	$1.99	—	—	—
Flour, white, 5 lb	Baking	$4.69	$2.43	$1.55	—
Flour, whole wheat, 5 lb	Baking	$4.69	$2.79	—	$1.94
Garlic powder, 2.5 oz	Baking	$2.99	—	—	—
Honey, 12 oz	Baking	$3.69	—	—	—
Honey, 16 oz	Baking	—	$3.49	—	—
Honey, 24 oz	Baking	—	—	$3.79	—
Mustard, ground, 0.46 oz	Baking	$1.99	—	—	—
Oats, quick, 18 oz	Baking	$2.99	—	—	—
Olive oil, extra virgin, 500 ml	Baking	$6.99	—	$4.29	$4.78
Olive oil, extra virgin, 1 L	Baking	$12.99	—	—	—
Sugar, white, 5 lb	Baking	$3.99		$1.89	$3.18
Sugar, brown, 24 oz	Baking	$2.99	$1.65	$1.19	$1.44
Vanilla extract, 4 oz	Baking	$10.99	—	—	—
Vegetable oil, 32 oz	Baking	$3.69	—	—	—
Vegetable oil, 48 oz	Baking	—	$4.18	$2.29	—
Vinegar, white, 32 oz	Baking	$5.69	$1.48	$0.79	$0.96

Product	Aisle	Whole Foods	Cub Foods	Aldi	Walmart
Salt	Baking	—	$0.54	$0.33	—
Butter, 1 lb	Dairy	$6.19	$2.79	$1.99	$2.28
Cheese, block cheddar, 8 oz	Dairy	$4.49	$2.49	$1.99	$2.44
Cheese, block mozzarella, 8 oz	Dairy	$4.49	$2.49	$1.99	$2.44
Cheese, block Swiss, 8 oz	Dairy	$5.49	$2.49	$2.49	$3.18
Cream cheese, 8 oz	Dairy	$1.69	$1.49	$0.99	$1.27
Eggs, one dozen	Dairy	$2.99	$1.43	$1.28	$1.56
Milk, skim, one gallon	Dairy	$3.99	$2.69	$2.29	$2.50
Sour cream, 16 oz	Dairy	$2.99	$2.04	$0.99	$0.96
Yogurt, vanilla, 32 oz	Dairy	$2.99	—	$1.59	$2.38
Cheese, block, Parmesan, 1 lb	Dairy	$12.99	—	—	—
Broccoli, frozen, 1 lb	Frozen	$1.69	$1.39	$0.99	$0.98
Cauliflower, frozen, 10 oz	Frozen	$2.69	$1.39	—	—
Corn, canned	Frozen	$0.99	—	$0.49	$0.68
Corn, frozen, 1 lb	Frozen	$1.69	$1.50	$0.95	$0.98
Orange juice, concentrate	Frozen	$3.69	$1.59	$1.25	$1.22
Peas, frozen, 16 oz	Frozen	$1.69	$1.50	$0.95	$0.98
Applesauce, 24 oz	Jarred & Canned	$2.99	$1.83	$0.95	$1.08
Artichoke hearts, canned	Jarred & Canned	$2.49	$2.29	—	—
Soup, cream of chicken, 14.5 oz	Jarred & Canned	$2.69	—	$0.49	—
Kalamata olives, jarred, 4.8 oz	Jarred & Canned	$3.39	—	—	—
Lemon juice, concentrate, 16 oz	Jarred & Canned	$4.69	$2.99	—	—
Mayonnaise, 32 oz	Jarred & Canned	$3.69	$2.69	$1.99	$2.87

Product	Aisle	Whole Foods	Cub Foods	Aldi	Walmart
Peanut butter, 18 oz	Jarred & Canned	$1.99	$2.35	—	$1.58
Salsa, jarred, 16 oz	Jarred & Canned	$3.38	$2.35	—	$1.54
Salsa, jarred, 24 oz	Jarred & Canned	—	$2.98	$1.49	—
Soup base, chicken, 8 oz	Jarred & Canned	$5.69	$3.04	—	—
Soy sauce, 10 oz	Jarred & Canned	$2.39	$1.25	—	—
Tomato paste, 6 oz	Jarred & Canned	$0.99	$0.73	$0.39	$0.46
Tomato sauce, 8 oz	Jarred & Canned	$0.99	$0.53	$0.25	$0.24
Tomatoes, canned, diced, 14.5 oz	Jarred & Canned	$1.39	$1.13	$0.49	$0.54
Worcestershire sauce, 5 oz	Jarred & Canned	$5.69	—	—	—
Worcestershire sauce, 10 oz	Jarred & Canned	—	$1.59	—	—
Ketchup, 24 oz	Jarred & Canned	—	$1.25	—	$1.23
Ketchup, 14 oz	Jarred & Canned	$1.69	$1.49	—	—
Mustard, prepared, 16 oz	Jarred & Canned	$1.99	$1.15	—	—
Spaghetti sauce, jarred, 26 oz	Jarred & Canned	—	$1.50	$0.99	—
Bacon, 1 lb	Meats	$4.99	$3.99	—	$2.98
Ground beef, 85/15, 1 lb	Meats	$2.99	$3.49	$2.49	$2.82
Chicken breast, fresh, boneless, 1 lb	Meats	$5.99	$3.19	—	$2.80
Ham, fresh, 1 lb	Meats	$7.99	$2.49	$1.49	—
Turkey, frozen, 1 lb	Meats	—	$1.68	$0.99	$1.18
Chicken breast, frozen, 3 lb	Meats	—	$5.97	$6.49	$6.48

Product	Aisle	Whole Foods	Cub Foods	Aldi	Walmart
Couscous, 1 lb.	Pasta & Grains	$1.99	—	—	—
Pasta, whole-wheat macaroni, 1 lb	Pasta & Grains	$2.99	$1.45	—	$1.28
Lentils, dried, 1 lb	Pasta & Grains	$1.99	$1.89	—	—
Quinoa, 1 lb	Pasta & Grains	$2.99	—	—	—
Rice, white, long grain, 2 lb	Pasta & Grains	$3.39	$2.88		$1.58
Rice, brown, 2 lb	Pasta & Grains	$3.39	$2.23	—	$1.88
Pasta, whole-wheat spaghetti, 16 oz	Pasta & Grains	$1.99	$1.45	—	$1.28
Chickpeas, dried, 1 lb	Pasta & Grains	$1.69	$1.59	—	—
Beans, pintos, dried, 2 lb	Pasta & Grains	—	—	$1.59	$1.82
Beans, pintos, dried, 1 lb	Pasta & Grains	$1.39	$1.74	—	—
Beans, black, dried, 1 lb	Pasta & Grains	$1.69	$1.19	—	—
Beans, kidneys, dried, 1 lb	Pasta & Grains	$1.69	$2.49	—	—
Apples, 3 lb	Produce	$5.99	$2.50	$2.50	$3.00
Bananas, 1 lb	Produce	$0.79	$0.69	$0.45	$0.67
Broccoli, fresh, 1 lb	Produce	$2.99	$2.29	$1.29	$1.58
Carrots, 5 lb	Produce	$3.99	$3.89	—	—
Carrots, 2 lb	Produce	—	$1.99	$0.99	$1.58
Carrots, 1 lb	Produce	$0.99	$0.99	—	—
Cauliflower, fresh, one head	Produce	$3.99	$3.49	$1.49	$2.68
Celery, 1 lb	Produce	$1.99	$1.69	$0.99	$1.36
Cilantro, fresh, one bunch	Produce	$1.99	$0.59	—	$0.78

Product	Aisle	Whole Foods	Cub Foods	Aldi	Walmart
Cucumbers, fresh, 1 lb	Produce	$2.99	$0.68/ea	—	$0.82/ea
Grapes, 1 lb	Produce	$2.99	$2.29	—	$2.28
Grapes, 2 lb	Produce	—	$2.29	$1.99	—
Garlic, fresh, 1 lb	Produce	$1.99	$1.99	—	$2.68
Lettuce, romaine, 1 lb	Produce	$2.49	$1.49	—	$1.50
Mushrooms, fresh, 8 oz	Produce	$2.49	$1.50	—	$1.50
Parsley, fresh, one bunch	Produce	$1.49	$0.59	—	$0.67
Potatoes, fresh, 5 lb	Produce	$5.99	$3.49	—	—
Potatoes, fresh, 10 lb	Produce	—	—	$2.99	$4.97
Spinach, fresh, 5 oz. bag	Produce	$1.99	$2.50	$1.99	$3.18
Onions, 3 lb	Produce	—	$3.99	$1.29	$2.18

CREATE YOUR PRICE BOOK. Traditionally frugal shoppers think of a price book as a small spiral notebook that can tuck nicely into a purse. If you go with this method, each page corresponds with a different product that you buy regularly. The most important information you can capture in your price book is the price of the product as well as the store in which it was purchased, plus the size of the item, the price per ounce, the date purchased, and even the brand name. How detailed you make your book is up to you, but the more information you have, the better armed you are to find bargains.

$ **USE A SPREADSHEET.** While a notebook works well, using a format such as Excel is even better. It allows you to update your entries easily; and you can simplify the process greatly by creating an Excel function to automatically calculate the cost per ounce of any given item. (Since product sizes often vary, knowing the price per ounce is the most accurate reflection of something's true cost.)

Here's the function to use when calculating price per ounce:

WAREHOUSE STORE PRICE COMPARISONS

	Cost	Ounces	Price Per Ounce
Extra virgin olive oil	$14.87	67.6	=B3/C3
Vegetable oil, 5 qt	$7.87	160	=B4/C4
White rice, 25 lb	$11.88	400	=B5/C5

If you have a PDA or Smartphone (such as a Palm or Black-Berry), you can even upload your spreadsheet for easy reference when you're shopping.

MORE PRICE BOOK TIPS

$ **PICK YOUR TOP FIFTY.** To make the process as easy as possible, start your price book with fifty products your family uses most often (if you've already created a grocery list spreadsheet as suggested on page 26, you're already halfway there).

$ **CHOOSE TO RECORD WHAT YOU ACTUALLY USE.** To get a good idea of which items to include, just look at what's currently in your refrigerator, freezer, and pantry. This is the best method because you can note the size of each product as you add it to the list.

USE YOUR RECEIPTS AS YOUR GUIDE. Save your grocery store register receipts for a period of time and compile a list based on your purchase history. One drawback of doing it this way is that most receipts will not include the size of the product—vital information if comparing price per ounce.

KEEP IT UP TO DATE. Each time you purchase an item in your price book, note the current cost. You'll find that you quickly become more cognizant of prices, and price increases and fluctuations will become obvious to you. It will also become obvious to you that advertised sales aren't always the best bargains. You'll see that some stores' everyday prices are lower than sale prices at other stores.

KEEP TRACK OF THE BRAND YOU BUY. Including the brand names of products in your price book can be advantageous, especially if you prefer one brand over another. That way, you can evaluate whether buying a name brand is worth paying the extra money, or in some cases you may notice that the brand name doesn't cost much more (if anything) than the generic counterpart.

STICK WITH IT. The longer you log grocery store prices, the greater the resource your spreadsheet becomes. If you save your information over the course of a year, your price book will allow you to take advantage of seasonal bargains.

💲 **MANY HANDS MAKE LIGHT WORK.** To make light work of the price book, share the work with several friends in your community who are also interested in the same information. Assign each person a specific store category (see chapter 2 for more information) and items to track. Once each of you has completed the assigned list, merge your information into one complete spreadsheet.

As you build your price book over several months, your entries will slow down. You'll notice that some prices don't vary by much, while others vary greatly. Those items will need to be updated on a regular basis, but it still won't take much time once the initial work has been done.

Here are some variations on the price book theme that might help you save even more money:

💲 **USE YOUR PRICE BOOK TO TRACK THE PRICE OF COMPLETE MEALS.** When you have already recorded prices of individual ingredients, computing the cost of meals is a cinch.

💲 **USE YOUR PRICE BOOK TO TRACK INVENTORY.** Add a column in your price book that lists how much of the product you have on hand and use as a pantry/freezer inventory.

💲 **USE YOUR PRICE BOOK AS A CUSTOMIZED GROCERY LIST.** Stick your price book spreadsheet on your refrigerator with a magnet and circle items as you run out of them. When you go to the store, simply grab your sheet and you have a ready-to-go grocery list.

"I decided to use Excel to track prices because it allows me to easily sort and calculate my data. My spreadsheet tracks the following: item description, product type, price, bonus buy (sale price), actual price, date purchased, and store. I enter the data from my grocery store receipts each week. I have been very surprised at how much I've been overpaying on certain things at the grocery store. I'm not saving as much as I thought on the weekly sale items. It took me a matter of minutes to set up my spreadsheet, and it takes ten or fifteen minutes to enter the data from my receipts each week. It's definitely worth the time. My only regret is that I didn't start shopping with a price book sooner!"

—LINDA MERRELL, HAGERSTOWN, MARYLAND

SHOP SMARTER: GROCERY SHOPPING STRATEGIES

Learning to navigate the store aisles and knowing which savings tools are available will help make it easy to stretch your food budget even further. Being a well-informed shopper puts you in a position to make the smartest decisions for your family.

Crack the Supermarket Marketing Tricks

Marketers have researched consumer buying habits and capitalized on them, and the supermarket is no exception. Being aware of their techniques can help you become a savvy shopper. Here's what you need to know:

DON'T ASSUME THE ITEMS ON THE ENDCAPS ARE ON SALE. Endcaps, or "gondolas," are the displays at the end of the aisles where the shelves meet. It's prime real estate in the supermarket. However, even if the bright red pricing looks as if it's a bargain—it may not be. Buy the item in the middle of the aisle where you can compare pricing to other products.

LOOK UP AND DOWN. If you want low prices, look lower on the shelves. More expensive brands invest in buying product placement. One case where this may not be true is where products are marketed to kids (fruit snacks, sugared cereals, etc.). These products tend to be placed lower on the shelves, where little eyes can see them best.

NOTICE COLORS OF LABELS. The more colorful a label is, the more expensive the packaging was to produce. Food labels with just two or three colors are often less expensive than products in full-color packaging.

DIG A LITTLE DEEPER FOR THE FRESHEST PRODUCTS. Older merchandise often gets pushed to the front to get rid of it more quickly. When it comes to buying dairy, meat, and produce, sometimes digging a little deeper will yield fresher products.

FLIER ITEMS AREN'T ALWAYS SALE ITEMS. Don't assume that if a product makes it to your grocery store ad, it is on sale. Sometimes products advertised are not on sale at all. Track your frequently purchased items by keeping a price book (as mentioned in chapter 1). That way you'll know when to stock up.

TEN FOR $10 DOESN'T REQUIRE PURCHASING TEN. Most supermarkets use this marketing strategy to encourage you to stock up. However, in many cases you'll get the same discounted price if you buy just one. If you're not sure what your store's policy is, be sure to ask.

$ **LOOK FOR "LOSS LEADERS."** Loss leaders usually appear on the front page of the supermarket circular and sometimes on the back. They're given the name because the store discounts them heavily and takes a "loss" on them to draw customers in, hoping that while they're there they will buy items with a higher profit margin to offset the loss. One clue that an item is a loss leader is if the store limits the number you can purchase.

$ **PAY CLOSE ATTENTION TO PACKAGE SIZES.** Some companies are making their products smaller—usually by an amount that you might not notice just by looking—to save costs on shipping or to boost profits. Most stores these days list the unit pricing for you. In order to really compare prices, look at the unit cost vs. the cost of the entire package. If you add a coupon in the mix, it gets more difficult to know automatically which product is a better buy.

$ **CARRY A CALCULATOR WITH YOU** to the store to calculate the cost per ounce or unit price so you can make a well-informed buying decision.

"When shopping, I use my cell phone's calculator feature to compare per-unit costs. For example, I'll often use it to figure out how much a can of pop costs in a 12-pack versus buying a case [24-pack]."
—MIKE SCHMITT, NORTH MANKATO, MINNESOTA

$ **GET THE MOST OUT OF LOYALTY PROGRAMS.** Loyalty programs are marketed to you as a way to save money. However, grocers know that instead of helping you save, they're getting you to spend more in the process. Research has found that stores that offer frequent shopper cards generally have higher markups than stores that don't. Use your price book to determine whether these loyalty programs work in your favor.

SHOP THE PERIMETER OF THE STORE FOR BASICS. There's a reason why the meat, eggs, milk, and other staples are located so far from the entrance. Supermarket designers lay out the basics along the perimeter to get customers who stop in to pick up a few things to pass by other tempting foods, linger just a bit longer, and pick up a few things that weren't on the list. Stick to the perimeter of the store for basics and you'll save more (and get out of the store quicker).

LOOK FOR STORE LAYOUT CHANGES. Supermarkets frequently move things around on the shelves or within the store. It's a process known as "resetting," and it's designed to get you to linger longer in their store, or to get you to try new products (often with a higher price tag) when you can't find the one you usually buy. Be aware of how these changes may be affecting your spending.

ASK FOR RAIN CHECKS OR REPLACEMENT ITEMS. If a sale item isn't available, ask for a rain check or something of equal value as a substitute. According to the website consumeraffairs.com, "grocery stores are the only retailers required to offer rain checks, unless the advertisement clearly states that quantities are limited, or unless the store can establish that advertised items were ordered in time for delivery and were in sufficient quantities to meet the public's reasonably anticipated demand." A rain check must be honored within sixty days of it being issued to a consumer, the Federal Trade Commission says. If the out-of-stock item is still not available, the supplier must notify the consumer holding the rain check of other options. Please note that some stores, most notably Jewel, limit rain checks to thirty days, so make sure to check your store's policy.

TIME IS OF THE ESSENCE. Get in and get out. The more time you spend lingering, the more you'll spend. Ever notice there aren't any clocks in the store, and they play soothing music that will relax you and lure you into staying even longer? It's there for a reason. Also, watch out for stand-alone displays that act as "speed bumps" along your way. They're there to distract you and get you to slow down.

Rethink How You Shop to Maximize Savings

Sometimes finding bargains requires you to step outside of the box. Leaving behind the comfort zone of your old habits and changing the way you view the products you buy can help you save even more.

CHOP, SLICE, AND SHRED IT YOURSELF. While most of us realize this is true with veggies, this also includes cheeses (grate it yourself) and meats. It's much more economical to buy a chunk of meat in the meat case and slice it yourself than to buy deli products. Sometimes, if you bring it to the deli counter, they'll even slice it for you.

$ **MIX IT AT HOME.** Most of us are aware that fruit juice concentrate is more economical than buying premixed juices. But don't forget that there are plenty of other mixtures, such as sauces, that can be made more affordably if you're willing to mix them yourself. For example, buying a packet of taco seasoning is cheaper than buying the boxed taco dinner kit. Better yet, make the mix from scratch yourself (see page 194) with spices you already have at home.

$ **LEARN TO READ LABELS.** Avoid foods with an excessive amount of preservatives, additives, and fillers. Know what you're getting for your money so you can make an educated buying decision. Sometimes it's worth it to spend a little bit more on a high-quality item. (See pages 92–93 on reading labels.)

$ **BE FLEXIBLE ABOUT BRANDS.** If you run out of coffee, do you automatically reach for Starbucks, or would you also consider Maxwell House? Being open to trying store brands and sale items is a great way to save money.

$ **USE PRICE-MATCHING STRATEGIES.** Does your grocery store match the sale prices of its local competitors? If you don't know, find out by simply asking an employee. Using a price-matching strategy can help you avoid spending extra time and gas to cash in on bargains from multiple stores.

$ **SHOP FOR MEALS,** not single ingredients; otherwise, it's a virtual certainty you'll end up at the store again later on.

HAVE RECIPES ON STANDBY. Keeping a list of standby recipes in your car or stored in your phone or PDA can help you out in a pinch if you find yourself at the supermarket without a list based on a menu plan.

"For those instances when you do not have a grocery list, set the timer. The more time you spend in the grocery store, the more you will throw in your cart. So if you normally spend sixty minutes shopping, allow yourself forty minutes. You will be less likely to browse for things you do not really need, like the junk food aisle, and more time getting the things that you do need because of the set time limit."

—JONI HEARD, MICANOPY, FLORIDA

LOOK BEYOND THE GROCERY STORE. Warehouse clubs, bakery outlets, dollar stores, and even pharmacies offer competitive prices on certain grocery items. Familiarizing yourself with prices, learning to spot a deal, and working these stores into your weekly shopping routine can help you save.

FOCUS ON FOOD AT THE GROCERY STORE. Things like diapers, cosmetics, shampoo, deodorant, and other toiletries are generally cheaper at places like Walgreens, CVS, or big-box retailers like Target and Walmart. CNN reports that grocery stores typically price non-food items 20 to 40 percent higher than other stores do. Buying them elsewhere also helps you keep tabs on your true grocery budget by making it easier to separate food costs from other household expenses.

DON'T AUTOMATICALLY BUY IN BULK. Buying in bulk isn't a good deal if your family can't use up the food before it spoils. Plus, studies have found that when we buy in bulk we often consume in bulk (suggested viewing: Brian Wansink on YouTube). If you're aiming to eat more fruits and vegetables, consuming them more often may be good for your diet, but obviously this can be a dangerous tactic to use with calorie-laden snacks and treats. Even if the price per ounce is lower for the large package, buying the small package is sometimes a better decision in the long run.

CHECK THE ETHNIC FOOD AISLES. In some supermarkets, the ethnic food aisles are loaded with grocery bargains. In fact, some of the same bags of rice, beans, and other foods cost less here than in the regular aisles. It's also a great way to experiment with inexpensive new food categories and add variety to your meal plan.

BE ON THE LOOKOUT FOR REGISTER ERRORS. Since it is estimated that up to $2.5 billion per year is made in scanning errors, it can pay to watch the scanner as your purchases are rung up. If you notice a mistake on your bill, be sure to speak up. Some stores even offer a "get it for free" policy on register mistakes under a certain dollar amount.

AVOID IMPULSE SHOPPING AT THE SUPERMARKET

Studies show that over half of the things that people buy at the supermarket are impulse buys, defined as things that weren't on the list when the customer entered the store. According to Paco Underhill in *Why We Buy: The Science of Shopping*, a full two-thirds of supermarket purchases are unplanned.

Impulse items aren't just the sodas, magazines, and candy in the checkout aisle. Supermarket gurus are cleverer than that. They place complementary products close to each other on the shelves—need some marshmallows to go with that hot chocolate? Some biscotti to go with your coffee? Watch out for temptations within the aisle as well.

BRING CASH. Only bring the amount of cash you intend to spend. Studies have found that consumers spend more, sometimes up to twice as much, when given the option to put it on plastic with a credit card. Avoid the urge to spend more and opt for a cash-only strategy. This is a *must* for shoppers who have a hard time sticking to a list. Carrying a limited amount of cash with you helps immediately discern the difference between wants and needs.

SORT PURCHASES IN YOUR CART. Put all unplanned purchases into the front part of your cart where the baby seat is. At the end of your trip, take a second look at what's in your cart and ask yourself if you really should be buying those items. If they're a great deal you simply can't pass up, keep them. If not, consider putting them back.

HAVE IT DELIVERED. If impulse purchases are an ongoing problem for you, take advantage of delivery and pickup services if your supermarket offers them. Staying out of the store separates you from temptation and helps you save on your food bill. See pages 81–83 for services that provide grocery home delivery in your area.

SHOP ON A FULL STOMACH. Everything looks appealing when you're hungry, making impulse purchases hard to resist. The best time to shop is after a full meal. Keep a stash of granola bars in your car to ward off hunger pangs in case you haven't had time to eat before shopping.

SKIP THE CART. If you can get by without a cart, opt for a basket instead. Less room means less space to put items you really don't need. If you're running in for a few things only, skip the basket and just carry what you need. Not only is there less space for storing your items, but the weight of carrying it around the store prompts you to get out quickly.

HAVE A CHECKOUT STRATEGY. It's no accident that impulse items are placed right near the checkout lanes, where the supermarket has a captive audience while customers wait in line. It's also no accident that these items have some of the highest markups storewide. To avoid being tempted, focus your attention elsewhere. Be prepared with a strategy. Use your time to organize your coupons, work on a to-do list, text a friend, or work on a crossword puzzle you keep in your purse.

FIND A NEW HOBBY. For many people, shopping is an enjoyable experience, to the point where it becomes a hobby. They find themselves at the supermarket several times a week "just browsing." If this describes you, try to channel your love of shopping to something more budget-friendly (such as cooking frugal meals from scratch).

Coupons 101

Coupons are a savings method that has been a part of our history for over one hundred years. The first grocery coupon dates back to 1895, when C.W. Post gave out tickets good for one cent off its new cereal, Grape Nuts. While today's technology is rapidly changing how coupons are printed and redeemed, they remain a cornerstone of many money-saving strategies.

Using coupons doesn't have to be an all-or-nothing proposition. Many people avoid coupons altogether because they think it's a lot of work, and that's simply not the case. You don't have to emulate the habits of the television coupon queen who slashed her grocery bill by 90 percent to enjoy the benefits of coupons. Clip as many or as few as is easy for you...or even enlist the help of your kids, which can be a great way to introduce them to frugality.

SKEPTICAL? TRY THE HALF-HOUR CHALLENGE. Devote a half hour each week to coupons and see how much money you save. You'll need just fifteen minutes for clipping coupons and fifteen minutes for matching the coupons you find to items already on sale at your store. Start by using coupons for the products you would normally buy anyway. If you're feeling like you can tackle more, branch out to coupons with large face values or for products you'd like to try. If, after one month and investing approximately two hours, you're not convinced you can save with clipping coupons, you can try another saving strategy.

"When shopping, I take my time and look at prices on everything. Many times a generic product is still less than a name-brand item on sale with a coupon. I only buy what we need. Just because we can get a good deal on junk food doesn't mean we buy it."

—KIMBERLY GIFFEN, TACOMA, WASHINGTON

WHERE TO FIND THE BEST COUPONS

Coupons aren't just found in the Sunday paper anymore. Even though the traditional free standing insert still accounts for nearly 90 percent of coupons clipped today, it's just one of many good resources available to shoppers.

MAKE USE OF PRINTABLE COUPON WEBSITES. Online coupons are more popular than ever. Shoppers printed $57 million in savings from the Coupons.com publisher network in March 2009, an increase of $38 million, or 192 percent, from the same month in 2008. Coupons.com and other sites devoted to bringing you online coupons in one place make it easier than ever to download and print. To get started, simply download the coupon printer software, select the coupons you want by checking the box on each one, then hit your print button.

Coupons are restocked frequently, so check back on a daily basis for the best selection. Most coupons you see online have print limits (for example: once 10,000 coupons have been printed, the coupon is no longer available). If you see one you can use, print it right away. It may be your only chance.

Notable sites include:

- ⓢ Coupons.com
- ⓢ Redplum.com
- ⓢ Coolsavings.com
- ⓢ Smartsource.com

ⓢ **MANUFACTURER WEBSITES.** Don't forget to visit the websites of brands you buy on a regular basis for promotions, special offers, and even coupons. If they have a mailing list, sign up and you may get coupons sent to you by mail.

ⓢ **GROCERY STORE WEBSITES.** The websites of your local grocery stores are another great source for coupons. Kroger, Cub Foods, Jewel-Osco, Safeway, Vons, and warehouse retailer BJs are just a few among many stores that are beginning to offer customers printable coupons. Some are printables; others are electronic discounts linked to your customer loyalty cards.

ⓢ **RETAIL AND PHARMACY WEBSITES.** Stores such as CVS, Walgreens, and Kmart also offer manufacturers' printable coupons on their websites. Check the sites of the stores you visit most often.

ⓢ **OVER THE PHONE.** Call the toll-free number printed on the products you buy regularly. Often manufacturers will send you coupons in the mail if you inquire about their availability.

COMPANY PUBLICATIONS. Sign up for company publications online. Many times, they're stocked with great coupons. Kraft's *Food and Family* magazine is a great example. Sign up online by visiting www.kraftfoods.com.

CATALINAS. These highly targeted coupons, which print out along with your grocery receipt, are based on information from the barcodes of the products you just purchased. For example, if you just bought a carton of ice cream, the Catalina may print a coupon for chocolate syrup or a competing brand of ice cream.

CHECKOUT REGISTER TAPE. When you get a receipt from the supermarket, don't forget to look on the back for coupons. These are usually local coupons good for money off a service such as dry cleaning, haircuts, or oil changes. Some register tapes also invite customers to call a toll-free number to complete a brief survey on their shopping experience. A quick one- or two-minute call could yield a coupon for a product worth a couple of dollars, which is definitely worth the time.

COUPON DISPENSERS. The red coupon dispensers put out by SmartSource known as "blinkies" dispense coupons in the grocery aisle right next to the product itself.

MAGAZINES, especially women's-interest magazines, often include coupons inside. Before you discard old magazines, check for discounts. *All You* magazine has more than your typical magazine. Most issues include at least $20 in coupons, which make it well worth the cover price. Many libraries also offer a magazine swap where you can take magazines and leave ones you've already read behind. Or visit discount magazine websites like www.bestdealmagazines.com or www.valuemags.com.

NEWSPAPERS. Not just in the Sunday circulars, coupons can also be found within the body of the newspaper as well in advertisements any day of the week. If you do use a lot of coupons from the Sunday insert, buy an extra newspaper and save even more. Look for extra copies of your Sunday paper at your dollar store during the week.

STORE CIRCULARS. Always look through your grocery store circular for coupons to use in-store. If they aren't delivered to you in the newspaper, most are available in your store's entryway.

PRODUCT PACKAGING. Look on cans, boxes, bottles, and inside the labels of things right in your own home. They may include coupons for savings off a future purchase.

FREE SAMPLES. By signing up for free samples online, you may also get valuable coupons sent to you by mail. When products are being sampled at your supermarket, there are frequently coupons being given away at the same time. Be sure to look.

COUPON SWAP BOXES. Sometimes you'll find these swap boxes inside the grocery store itself. Libraries are also common places to find them. Search for coupons you need, and leave the ones you don't need behind for others to enjoy.

COUPON EXCHANGES. Start an exchange with other interested members at a local playgroup, church, or at work. You can even take your swapping online. At Mommysavers.com, members post their ISO (in search of) lists as well as their FT (for trade) lists at http://mommysavers.com/boards/coupon-trading.

JOIN A COUPON TRAIN. A coupon train is an envelope filled with non-expired coupons that is sent between participants, or "riders," of the train. A member receives the "train" in the mail and removes the coupons she can use. She then replaces those coupons with coupons she has no use for and sends it on to the next "rider" on the mailing list. To join a train, visit the Mommysavers.com coupon forums.

PAYING FOR COUPONS. It's important to note that in most cases, paying for a manufacturer's coupon is illegal. However, paying for the time it takes someone to clip the coupon and mail it to you is not. Because of this loophole, dozens of websites as well as eBay sellers are offering their "services" to provide coupons to willing buyers at a price. Before joining a group like this, consider whether it's worth the expense and effort to get something that is typically available to you free of charge.

"As an avid coupon clipper, I decided to give coupon trains a try as a way to get more coupons without having to buy an extra paper. On the Mommysavers.com coupon trains, each of the four 'riders' provides a wish list of coupons they want: baby products, food, cleaning products, etc. Being on several trains allows me to truly take advantage of sales. Since I have multiple coupons of the things I need, I can stock up for less. The ones I don't need get passed along to others who do want them. I can give a Pampers coupon that I don't need and in return find coupons for granola bars that I need."

—LEIGHANN PATTERSON, LAKEWOOD, OHIO

The average face value of coupons distributed in 2008 was $1.44. The average value of coupons redeemed was $1.09.

SOURCE: COUPONINFONOW.COM

ORGANIZING COUPONS

Making coupons easy to file and easy to use is a key to your success. A coupon system can be anything from a simple white envelope to an elaborate folder. The important thing is to find a system that works well for you and your personal coupon usage.

KEEP IT SIMPLE. If you're just getting started with coupons and only clip a few each week, a simple white envelope you tuck in your purse may be all you need.

PORTABLE PLASTIC. Plastic coupon caddies and accordion organizers can be found at just about any big-box retailer in the office supply section. Some are created specifically for coupons; others are for sorting bills. This is the most popular choice because of its portability—it's easy to throw in your purse and go.

INDEX CARD BOXES. Plastic index card boxes that you'd use for recipe cards work well for sorting coupons too. They come with tabbed dividers that make dividing them by category very easy. The drawback? They're not as portable.

THREE-RING BINDER. A three-ring binder with baseball card inserts is a popular method for die-hard coupon users because the see-through sheets make finding coupons at a glance very easy. Separate sections with tabbed dividers labeled with the grocery aisles. A pencil pouch with a calculator, scissors, and pen help make your job easier.

BREAK COUPONS INTO CATEGORIES. It helps to separate your coupons into the categories you use most often, such as canned goods, baby products, cereal, baking, dairy, etc. After serious coupon clipping for a few months, you will discover which categories work the best for you.

SORT BY DATE. Arranging coupons by expiration date can help you avoid forgetting about a coupon before it expires. Place the dates closest to expiration in the front, the longest in the back.

If there are coupons you need to use the next time you visit the store, pull them out and place in the front of your caddy.

$ **USE THAT FREE LABOR!** If your kids are old enough, have them cut and file coupons for you. Use the money you save toward something special you all can enjoy together.

MAXIMIZE YOUR COUPON SAVINGS

Clipping the best coupons is only the start. Knowing how and when to use them is another important part of your savings strategy.

$ **COMBINE COUPONS WITH TWO-FOR-ONES.** A lot of grocery stores also offer BOGO (buy one, get one free) sales. In this instance, you can use both the in-store coupon to get the BOGO deal and two manufacturer coupons (one for each item).

$ **FIND A STORE THAT WILL DOUBLE YOUR COUPONS.** If your town doesn't have one, it may be worth a short drive to another town to a store that does. Couponing.about.com has a state-by-state list of stores that will double your coupons. If you're making a special trip, be sure to call in advance to see if the store has restrictions on doubling coupons. Some stores will only double coupons under $0.50; some only double coupons on certain days of the week.

$ **BUY THE SMALLEST SIZE.** If you were paying attention on page 36, you'll remember that buying in bulk doesn't always save you money. This is also true when using a coupon. What you will need to consider is the price per ounce. Here is an example:

WITHOUT COUPON:

    Ketchup, 14 oz   Price: $1.25   *Cost per ounce: $0.09*

    Ketchup, 24 oz   Price: $1.99   *Cost per ounce: $0.08*

WITH COUPON:

    Ketchup, 14 oz   Price: $1.25 – $0.50 Coupon = $0.75

                                   Cost per ounce: $0.05

    Ketchup, 24 oz   Price: $1.99 – $0.50 Coupon = $1.49

                                   Cost per ounce: $0.06

While the price per ounce of the larger size is more economical without the coupon, the smaller size is the better buy *with* the coupon. Keep a small calculator in your purse (or use the calculator function on your cell phone) to help calculate the best deal.

BE WILLING TO TRY NEW THINGS. Many coupons are for items that are new to the marketplace, or for products you may not have tried before. By being willing to experiment with new things and giving up your brand loyalty, you can save quite a bit, and sometimes discover a new favorite product.

READ THE FINE PRINT. Sometimes you can use the coupon for more than just what's pictured on it. For example, a cereal coupon may be good for any type of Cheerios, not just Honey Nut Cheerios. Reading the fine print to determine what size and type of item the coupon is intended for can help you make smarter purchases.

KNOW WHEN NOT TO USE COUPONS. When is a coupon not a good deal? Knowing this can be as helpful to you as the coupon itself. In many cases, the generic or store-brand version of what you're buying is cheaper than the more expensive counterpart even *with* a coupon. Don't get caught up with how much the coupon allows you to save, but instead still look at what you're spending. For example, you may be saving $2.00 off a $4.00 item with a coupon, but you would have spent $1.89 on the private-label counterpart if you hadn't had the coupon at all.

YOUR SAVINGS CAN HELP. Have expired coupons? Don't throw them away! Military families stationed overseas can use them up to six months past their expiration date. Unfortunately, there isn't one central distribution point to send the coupons. Visit the Mommysavers.com coupon trading forum for a listing of bases that will accept them.

COMBINE COUPONS WITH IN-STORE SALES. Die-hard coupon users know that to truly maximize their savings, they need to pair coupons with in-store sales and promotions. Many websites and discussion forums exist to take the work out of it for you. Notable sites include:

- **COUPONMOM.COM** offers a "Virtual Coupon Organizer" that lists grocery deals state by state and which coupons to pair them with for the best deals.
- **GROCERYGAME.COM** is a subscription-based service that

costs $10 for an eight-week membership. Subscribe to stores in your area and get a list that sorts discounts by percentage savings.

‹ **MOMMYSAVERS.COM** members share the scoop on their local supermarket bargains and unadvertised specials, as well as which coupons they've paired them with, in the Grocery Bargains discussion forum. Membership is free.

HIGH-TECH SAVINGS

With newspaper readership trending down, new coupon technologies are emerging. Electronic discounts are the next big thing in coupon usage, offering several benefits over traditional coupons, including the ability to track redemption rates and capture customer demographic information. Not to mention that less paper is easier on the environment.

TEXT MESSAGE COUPONS. Coupons are now available via the Internet and sent to your mobile phone. To redeem them, simply open the text message and present it to the cashier. Log on to Cellfire.com and answer some basic questions along with your cell phone number and email address. Participation is free, but standard carrier fees will apply.

ELECTRONIC WIDGETS. More and more supermarkets are using advanced technology to attract and retain customers. The Meijer chain uses a downloadable computer program called Mealbox to help their customers build grocery lists around coupons and sale items. After perusing the bargains online, shoppers print out grocery lists with barcodes that are scanned at checkout for coupon savings. Visit http://shortcuts.com.

$ **SOCIAL NETWORKING SITES.** Online coupon supplier coupons.com even has applications on the social networking site Facebook. Simply add the application, and they'll instantly provide you with a selection of coupons for everyday products. They also have a Twitter feed that notifies followers of recently added coupons.

$ **UPROMISE.** Upromise makes it easy for parents to save money for their child's education by offering discounts at retailers that are automatically deposited into a special account. To save on groceries, simply register your grocery store card and select the discounts you're interested in. When you purchase a participating product using your store card, the savings will be deposited in your Upromise account automatically. Accumulated savings can be invested in 529 plans, used to pay down student loans, or received as a check for college expenses. To sign up for a free account, visit www.upromise.com.

SUPERMARKET LOYALTY PROGRAMS

A supermarket loyalty card can be another important grocery saving success. These little pieces of plastic, which typically resemble a credit or debit card or a keychain fob, are also known as rewards cards, points cards, advantage cards, or club cards. Customers present them at the checkout counter in order to receive product discounts.

HOW LOYALTY PROGRAMS WORK

Loyalty programs are currently being offered by about 45 percent of U.S. grocery retailers, according to the Food Marketing Institute (FMI).

Before you rely on a supermarket loyalty card to save money, it's important to understand how they work. Most offer discounts exclusively to consumers who use the card. For example, a box of cereal may cost $2.39 for someone without the card and $2.19 for someone with it. When you get to the checkout lane, the cashier scans your card in order for you to receive the discount.

For stores, it's a great way to profile their customers' buying patterns. When you use your card, your store now knows what you've purchased, how often you shop, and how much you spend. It's a great way for stores to collect data, and sometimes even sell it to market research companies. In some cases, stores even profit more by selling the data than they do on the products you've purchased.

The information gathered can benefit the customer as well. Loyalty card information is also used to send you special targeted offers and coupons. Information collected through loyalty cards can also be used to notify customers of product recalls, as was the case in a Sam Adams beer recall in April of 2008; information collected by Price Chopper's AdvantEdge loyalty cards was used to alert customers by phone of a potentially dangerous product.

The biggest criticism of customer loyalty cards is the invasion of privacy. For most customers, the discounts they enjoy are worth it. If you're weary about sharing your personal information, consider creating a "dummy" account. Most don't require your real name or address, so creating a card under an alias is perfectly acceptable.

Typically, stores that build loyalty discounts into their pricing strategies have slightly higher everyday prices than stores without them. However, if you've created a price book and learn to spot a deal, you can use loyalty discounts to find some terrific buys.

"I will usually only buy sale items when I shop. I will shop around and check all the local fliers to see which store has the best prices for that week. I try to match up my coupons to the sale items for the most savings if possible."

—MISSY STUYNISKI, JEWETT CITY, CONNECTICUT

$ **COUPON KIOSKS.** Shoppers at pharmacies like CVS and supermarkets like Giant Eagle are now able to scan their loyalty cards at special kiosks within the store to generate additional coupons and discounts. Discounts are based on past purchase history as well as additional unadvertised in-store specials.

$ **ELECTRONIC UPLOADS AND ECOUPONS.** When customers type in their loyalty card information online, they're eligible for additional discounts and coupons that are loaded onto their cards electronically. The discounts are then realized when the cashier scans the card and the eligible product at a subsequent store visit. These types of discounts are especially appealing because there's no clipping or organizing coupons involved. Shortcuts.com is one such portal for supermarkets like Kroger, Ralph's, Fry's, and more. Companies such as Proctor & Gamble and Unilever also offer ecoupons that can be loaded onto certain store cards. Check out www.pgesaver.com and www.softcoin.com/Sites/Unilever_MoreValue/Page/HomePage

$ **A CONSOLIDATED LOYALTY CARD.** If you have an extensive collection of loyalty cards, consider consolidating all of the bar codes into just one card. Just enter up to eight loyalty card barcodes and click the "create your card" button at www.justoneclubcard.com.

$ **CASHIER KINDNESS.** If you forget your loyalty card at home, ask the cashier to swipe a spare card for you.

Store Brand and Generic Products

Generic products first made their appearance during the recession of the 1970s as a cheaper food alternative to help consumers save money. The bland black-and-white packaging was indicative of the quality as well. Many generics were inferior cast-offs of a name-brand counterpart (such as tea dust instead of tea leaves), and for that reason, generics got a bad rap.

Today, store brands and private labels have emerged as a low-cost counterpart, but they're much different than the generics of an era past. According to AC Nielsen, they have a 25 percent market share in stores across the United States and are gaining market share over name brands each year. In Europe, private-label brands account for as much as 40 percent of the groceries sold.

INSTANT BARGAINS. When you purchase private-label brands, savings are instant. Stores are able to offer private-label foods at prices about 25 to 30 percent less than name brands because they don't have the hefty marketing, advertising, and market research expenses. Consumers love them because they often provide the same quality but at a much lower price.

YOU DON'T HAVE TO SACRIFICE QUALITY. Many private-label foods are manufactured at the same location as more expensive brands, with only slight variations so as to not infringe on copyright laws. Manufacturers want a piece of the pie—which is why they're helping stores supply them. However, most are tight-lipped about which products they produce. An investigation by Consumer Reports in 2005 found that companies like Alcoa (Reynold's Wrap), Bird's Eye, Chicken of the Sea, and McCormick Spices as well as Del Monte also produce private-label brands.

Ever notice that when name-brand foods are recalled, there is often a private-label food recalled as well? Those recalls can tip you off as to what foods are produced at the same locations as name-brand foods. For example, the peanut butter salmonella outbreak included both Peter Pan and Walmart's store brand. When comparing products, the best thing to do is simply read the labels. Often, you'll see the same ingredients listed in exactly the same order.

Stores like their own private-label brands because they offer a higher profit margin than do sales of national brands, sometimes 10 to 15 percent higher. They're also a key to customer loyalty. If you become a fan of a product that's only available at a certain store, it's more likely you'll return to purchase more things.

TAKE ADVANTAGE OF MONEY-BACK GUARANTEES. Since most stores offer a money-back guarantee on their own brands, you're carrying no risk to try them. If you're apprehensive, start out by trying frozen vegetables, pantry staples like flour and sugar, and other products with consistent flavors. Do a side-by-side blind taste test and let your taste buds be the judge.

DID YOU KNOW? The first generic products were introduced by Chicago Jewel stores in 1977.

SOURCE: CONSUMER AFFAIRS

WHERE TO SHOP FOR SAVINGS

There are important things besides prices to consider when deciding where to shop. Other aspects of shopping add value to you as a consumer, which is something to keep in mind. Among the questions to ask yourself:

- How far is it from my home?
- What is the quality of the merchandise like? Are meats high-quality? Is produce fresh?
- Does it have the items on my list? Will I only have to make one stop to get everything I need?
- Can I use coupons there?
- How quickly can I get in and out?
- Do they accept debit or credit cards or cash only?

Traditional Food Stores

Most grocery stores fall into a certain category: high-low stores, specialty markets, hypermarkets, and limited assortment stores (it's also possible for stores to be two categories at once). Other stores you typically don't think of as grocery stores sell food too—sometimes at great prices. Knowing which strategies work best at each store will help you find the best bargains.

HIGH-LOW STORES

Most traditional supermarkets fall under this category. Their pricing structure is based on offering customers regular sales and promotions. Their everyday prices are generally higher than other stores, but when items are on sale, prices are typically lower. Low profit margins on sale items are offset by customers purchasing non-sale items as well. Savvy shoppers can use this pricing strategy to their advantage by only purchasing items when they're on sale.

- **STUDY THE CIRCULARS.** These stores typically have the best weekly sales, so investing a few minutes to study the ads and plan your meals accordingly can help you save a lot.

- **BRING YOUR COUPONS.** This is a great place to use them, especially when you pair them with in-store sales.

SPECIALTY SUPERMARKETS

Specialty supermarkets draw customers who aren't as concerned with price as they are with other factors such as service, selection, and quality. Whole Foods, for example, attracts clientele who are interested in organic, natural foods. Other grocery stores may bag your groceries for you, have in-house coffee shops, and offer an expanded selection of gourmet items. In most cases, these stores have higher-than-average prices on what they do sell, but don't count them out completely. Some may follow a pricing structure (see below) that allows customers to find some hidden gems within their aisles.

$ **TIME IS MONEY.** If you're close to a specialty store, sometimes running in to pick up a few things will save you fifteen minutes and gas money. It's a money-wise decision, even if you have to pay a couple dollars more.

$ **KNOW YOUR PRICES.** The key to shopping at these stores is to familiarize yourself with pricing so you can spot a good deal and time your purchases accordingly.

HYPERMARKETS

Supermarkets within big-box retailers such as Walmart Supercenter and SuperTarget offer one-stop shopping, which makes them popular for the sake of convenience. Besides grocery stores, many offer eye centers, banks, and sometimes even hair salons. Because of their large size, typically 150,000 to 200,000 square feet, they're not exactly the best choice if you're in a hurry. However, Consumers' Checkbook, a nonprofit organization, found that hypermarkets like Walmart Supercenter and SuperTarget have lower overall prices than regular grocery chains (16 percent less in Seattle, 12 percent less in Chicago, and 10 percent less in San Francisco). Other hypermarkets include Meijer, Fred Meyer, and Super Kmart.

$ **MAP OUT YOUR LIST.** Since hypermarkets have the largest floor plan of any store, it's easy to waste time backtracking to get a forgotten item. Before you set foot in the store, arrange your list by department to make efficient use of your time.

USE HYPERMARKET COUPONS. SuperTarget has coupons on its website, www.supertarget.com, for a wide array of food products, including their popular private label, Archer Farms, as well as national brands. Because they're designated as store coupons, you can also use manufacturers' coupons in conjunction with them to save even more. Coupons for Target are also available on the website www.afullcup.com.

PRICE-MATCH. Walmart Supercenter offers a price-match guarantee, so it pays to bring along competitors' circulars. Please don't alienate the cashier: Keep all price-matching items together in your cart with the competitors' fliers to facilitate your transaction.

WHAT YOU NEED TO KNOW BEFORE YOU SHOP AT A WALMART SUPERCENTER:

- Store managers make the final decision in always taking care of customers, but they do have guidelines for matching the competition.
- They do honor "Preferred Shopping Card" advertised prices. The items must be like items, be advertised, and require a competitor's shopping card for the discount to apply.

- They do not honor advertisements that require a purchase in order to receive the advertised price or free product.
- They do not honor "Buy One Get One Free" advertisements.
- They do not honor double or triple coupons or percent-off advertisements.
- They do not honor other retailers' "misprinted" advertised prices.
- They do not honor Internet pricing.
- They do not honor competitors' advertisements from outside of the store's or club's local trade territory.

SOURCE: HTTP://WALMARTSTORES.COM/FACTSNEWS/7659.ASPX

LIMITED-ASSORTMENT STORES

Limited-assortment stores like Aldi and Save-a-Lot have gained popularity with the recent economic downturn because of their ability to offer a limited assortment of commonly purchased grocery staples at prices 30 to 50 percent less than other stores. By curtailing their product selection (Aldi stocks about 1,000 products, compared to about 25,000 at the typical supermarket) and offering a no-frills environment, they're able to slash overhead costs. Most of their product offerings are private-label brands. They work with manufacturers to secure the lowest prices on their own brands, which means consumers aren't supporting the advertising and marketing costs of national brands.

Aldi

Aldi is a discount grocery chain that originated in Germany and started its U.S. operations in 1976. It now operates in eighteen countries around the world. It has over 850 stores in the U.S. and is the 24th largest grocer in terms of gross sales—which is quite an accomplishment considering its small size.

Basics such as loaves of bread, pantry staples, milk, cheese, canned vegetables, and produce all typically cost less than supermarket non-sale prices.

Let's let the facts speak for themselves. A price comparison of things the average shopper would commonly buy shows that Aldi is on average 18 percent less than Walmart Supercenter and 22 percent less than a local grocery chain (Cub Foods). I compared Aldi's prices with the store-brand counterparts (or lowest cost alternative) at the other two stores. Although Walmart beat Aldi's prices several times, the overall low-cost winner was clear.

Product	Cub Foods	Walmart	Aldi
Baking soda	$0.69	$0.36	$0.43
Sugar, brown, 24 oz	$1.65	$1.44	$1.19
Vinegar, white, 32 oz	$1.48	$0.96	$0.79
Butter, 1 lb	$2.79	$2.28	$1.99
Cheese, block cheddar, 8 oz	$2.49	$2.44	$1.99
Cheese, block mozzarella, 8 oz	$2.49	$2.44	$1.99
Cheese, block Swiss, 8 oz	$2.49	$3.18	$2.49
Cream cheese, 8 oz	$1.49	$1.27	$0.99
Eggs, one dozen	$1.43	$1.56	$1.28

Product	Cub Foods	Walmart	Aldi
Milk, skim, one gallon	$2.69	$2.50	$2.29
Sour cream, 16 oz	$2.04	$0.96	$0.99
Broccoli, frozen, 1 lb	$1.39	$0.98	$0.99
Corn, frozen, 1 lb	$1.50	$0.98	$0.95
Orange juice, concentrate	$1.59	$1.22	$1.25
Peas, frozen, 16 oz	$1.50	$0.98	$0.95
Applesauce, 24 oz	$1.83	$1.08	$0.95
Mayonnaise, 32 oz	$2.69	$2.87	$1.99
Tomato paste, 6 oz	$0.73	$0.46	$0.39
Tomato sauce, 8 oz	$0.53	$0.24	$0.25
Tomatoes, canned, diced, 14.5 oz	$1.13	$0.54	$0.49
Ground beef, 85/15, 1 lb	$3.49	$2.82	$2.49
Turkey, frozen, 1 lb	$1.68	$1.18	$0.99
Chicken breast, frozen, 3 lb	$5.97	$6.48	$6.49
Apples, 3 lb.	$2.50	$3.00	$2.50
Bananas, 1 lb	$0.69	$0.67	$0.45
Broccoli, fresh, 1 lb	$2.29	$1.58	$1.29
Carrots, 2 lb	$1.99	$1.58	$0.99
Cauliflower, fresh, one head	$3.49	$2.68	$1.49
Celery, 1 lb	$1.69	$1.36	$0.99
Potatoes, fresh, 10 lb	$6.98	$4.97	$2.99
Spinach, fresh, 5 oz. bag	$2.50	$3.18	$1.99
Onions, 3 lb	$3.99	$2.18	$1.29
Total:	**$71.88**	**$60.42**	**$48.58**

The margins listed here may not seem big, but consider this. If you're accustomed to spending $500 per month on groceries, an overall savings of 16 percent (over Walmart Supercenter) would add up to $960 per year. A savings of 32 percent (over Cub Foods) would amount to $1,920 per year.

Here's what you need to know before you go:

- **LEAVE CHECKS AND CREDIT CARDS AT HOME.** Aldi only accepts cash and debit cards. They also do not accept manufacturers' coupons.

- **BRING YOUR CHANGE.** The carts are locked up outside the store, and you must "rent" one by depositing a quarter when you take it.

- **BRING YOUR BAGS.** They do provide grocery bags, but you must pay for them (paper bags are $0.05 and plastic bags are $0.10 each).

- **EMBRACE SURPRISE.** They stock "Special Purchase" items—good only while supplies last—that appeal to the shopper who likes the element of surprise.

- **TRY SOMETHING NEW.** Most of their prices are so low you can afford to take a chance on taste. They even offer a double money-back guarantee, which states they will replace the product in addition to refunding your money if it doesn't meet your expectations.

Trader Joe's

Trader Joe's is part limited-assortment store, part specialty market. Because it operates on a limited-assortment business model and offers its own private label (80 percent of goods are store brands), you'll find good-for-you foods from around the world at surprisingly low prices. They specialize in health-conscious foods with no artificial colors, flavors, MSG, trans fats, or genetically modified ingredients. No coupons are accepted.

GIVE CHUCK A TRY. Trader Joe's is widely known for its affordable Charles Shaw wine, priced at just $1.99 a bottle, aptly nicknamed "Two Buck Chuck" (sometimes "Three Buck Chuck" depending on the region in which it is sold).

TREAT YOURSELF FOR LESS. TJ's (what regulars call Trader Joe's) is great for foodies on a budget. If it's gourmet fare like imported cheeses and specialty meats you're after, this is a good place to find them at down-to-earth prices. Some folks report that fresh flowers are a great deal here as well, making it a great store to hit if you're throwing a dinner party or entertaining at home.

Stores are located in larger metropolitan areas only. To find a location near you, visit http://traderjoes.com.

"I like to make a cheese and cracker tray when we have friends over. The Trader Joe's cheeses are better and much less expensive than any other grocery stores. The last time I was there I picked out a wedge of aged gouda, an herbed goat cheese, and an aged English cheddar. My

bill was about $14. The same sized goat cheese at the regular grocery store costs $8.99 for just that!"

—DIANE LEVENE, GAITHERSBURG, MARYLAND

Think Outside the Box

Often the best food buys aren't at the grocery store at all. Thinking out of the box will help you cash in on the best deals when it comes to buying food for your family. Keeping a price book can help you know where the cheapest prices are for the foods you regularly buy.

BAKERY OUTLETS

Bakery outlets aren't just for bread. Besides products like bread, bagels, and buns, they also stock cookies, snacks, and other items.

CHECK EXPIRATION DATES. While the things you find there are typically just as fresh as—if not fresher than—those at the grocery store, it's important to check expiration dates. Most of the things you find there will freeze well, too.

VISIT BAKERY OUTLETS ON "BARGAIN" DAYS to save even more. To find an outlet near you, simply search the Internet using the terms "bakery outlet + [your city]." Here are several popular bakery outlets:

- Bimbo Bakeries: www.bimbobakeriesusa.com
- Entenmann's: http://entenmanns.gwbakeries.com/op-locator-Store-Outlet.cfm
- Wonder/Hostess: www.bakeryoutlets.com/storelocator.asp
- George Weston: www.gwbakeries.com/outlet.cfm
- Holsum: www.holsum.com/bakery.shtml

DOLLAR STORES

Food makes up between 12 and 25 percent of revenue at dollar stores, according to *Retailing Today*, and an ever-increasing segment of the population is incorporating dollar stores in its bargain-hunting routine. The big four brands are Dollar General, Family Dollar, Dollar Tree, and 99 Cent Only stores. The Dollar General and Family Dollar sell items of varied price points, while the Dollar Tree's merchandise is all $1.00 (or less). The 99 Cent Only store prices all its merchandise as its name implies, at $0.99. Product mix varies by store, with Dollar Tree focusing more on snacks and candy than the other three. Dollar stores are able to offer low prices because they purchase manufacturer overstocks, which also means their assortment is hit-or-miss.

§ **IF YOU SEE A BARGAIN, STOCK UP**—chances are you may not see it there again.

§ **DON'T GET LURED INTO THINKING EVERYTHING IS A BARGAIN.** Your local dollar store can be a great place to pick up inexpensive snacks, canned goods, cereal, beverages, and even spices. It's important to know your prices here, however, since not everything is a great deal. While food for $1 sounds like a steal, it can sometimes be found for less at your grocery store.

§ **BE WARY OF TEMPTATIONS.** When everything's a dollar, it's easy to rationalize purchases, even on the tightest of budgets. Stick to your list and leave the impulse purchases behind.

§ **PAY ATTENTION TO PACKAGE SIZES.** Name brands like Clorox, Colgate, and Tide can sometimes be found at dollar stores.

However, their sizes may be smaller than their regular grocery store counterparts, making it even more important to pay attention to the price per ounce.

LOOK BEYOND THE FOOD AISLE. Some of the best buys at dollar stores aren't food at all. Look for:

- Paper products
- Condiments
- Cleaning products
- Toiletry items
- Over-the-counter medications and pain relievers
- Food storage containers
- Snacks
- Gift wrap
- Kitchen gadgets and utensils

DOLLAR STORE/GROCERY STORE PRICE COMPARISONS

	Cost	Ounces	Price Per Ounce
Dollar store pink bismuth	$1.00	8	$0.125
Grocery store pink bismuth (store brand)	$2.23	8	$0.279
Dollar store milk of magnesia	$1.00	12	$0.083
Grocery store milk of magnesia (store brand)	$3.48	12	$0.290

	Cost	**Ounces**	**Price Per Ounce**
Dollar store acetaminophen, kids' liquid	$1.00	4	$0.250
Grocery store acetaminophen, kids' liquid (store brand)	$4.49	4	$1.123
Dollar store soap, bar, 3.2 oz. 2-pack	$1.00	6.4	$0.156
Grocery store soap, bar, 4.5 oz. 2-pack (least expensive brand)	$1.99	9	$0.221
Dollar store ketchup	$1.00	24	$0.042
Grocery store ketchup (store brand)	$1.19	24	$0.050
Dollar store vinegar, balsamic	$1.00	8.5	$0.118
Grocery store vinegar, balsamic	$3.69	16.9	$0.218
Dollar store salad dressing, ranch	$1.00	16	$0.063
Grocery store salad dressing, ranch (store brand)	$2.99	24	$0.125
Dollar store pine cleaner	$1.00	40	$0.025
Grocery store pine cleaner (store brand)	$2.19	28	$0.078
Dollar store laundry detergent, liquid	$1.00	30	$0.033
Grocery store laundry detergent, liquid (store brand)	$2.99	50	$0.060

FARMER'S MARKETS AND LOCAL OPTIONS

Local farmer's markets are a great source of affordable produce. While prices may be more expensive than traditional grocery stores, you need to keep in mind the other savings. The product will generally be superior in terms of flavor and nutrition, and you're supporting the local economy, plus eliminating the environmental cost of transporting the produce long distances. More ways to save:

- **PRESERVE SEASONAL GOODIES** by canning and freezing them for later use. When you find a bargain, stock up! (See page 220 for more on preserving, freezing, and canning.)

- **SHOP AROUND.** Prices at the farmer's market can vary quite a bit according to which booth/merchant you're looking at. It pays to shop around and wait before making your final purchase.

- **NEGOTIATE DISCOUNTS.** If all the other sellers are selling a bag of sweet corn for $4, you may be able to talk the merchant down from $5 to make the sale. Consider timing when negotiating the sale. If it's near the end of the day, the seller may be more likely to make a deal so he doesn't have to pack up the merchandise to take it home.

- **GET TO KNOW THE SELLERS.** Develop an ongoing relationship with sellers you do business with. You may be able to strike a deal with a seller by purchasing blemished produce at a reduced price. Ask them questions such as:

§ What products look the best this year?

§ Do you allow people to visit your farm to pick their own?

§ **YOU-PICK FARMS.** You can save even more if you pick the produce yourself. To locate a you-pick farm in your county, visit www.pickyourown.org.

§ **SUPPORT CSA (COMMUNITY SUPPORTED AGRICULTURE).** CSAs are a great way to save money and make a commitment to local farms and agriculture. Farms sell shares in their CSA program, usually on a yearly basis. In exchange for their share, members, or "shareholders," receive weekly baskets of a variety of fresh food, flowers, meat, eggs, and produce during the local growing season.

With over 2,200 CSAs in the United States, chances are there is one near you. To find one, visit the Local Harvest website: www.localharvest.org/csa

"When one of our local farmers became part of the Community Supported Agriculture (CSA), we decided to join. It has been a great experience for us. For $320 per year, we get $30 of produce each week for twenty weeks in the spring and summer. Do the math—that's a $600 value! The produce doesn't have the pesticides and added chemicals that conventional produce has, so I can feel safe in giving it to my kids. The taste is above and beyond what you buy in the store—I love their heirloom tomatoes!"

—TAMMY HARPER, NORTHERN CAMBRIA,
PENNSYLVANIA

§ **JOIN A BUYING CLUB.** A buying club is made up of a group of several people or families who pool their money to purchase organic and natural food from distributors collectively as a group. Because of their purchasing power, they gain access to wholesale distributors, eliminating the middleman, which is the grocery store or food co-op. They operate similarly to CSAs, where members get a share of the order placed, but instead they're purchasing from a distributor rather than the grower himself.

If you can't find a buying club in your area, consider starting one. Most successful groups start with five to eight families. For additional information, visit www.unitedbuyingclubs.com.

PHARMACIES

When you're at the grocery store, focus on food. Diapers, cosmetics, toiletries, cleaners, and other products are cheaper elsewhere, especially if you combine coupons and in-store rebate programs at pharmacies like Walgreens, CVS, and Rite Aid. In addition to their great buys on nonfood items, pharmacies also sell a small selection of groceries. While their grocery prices are usually higher, you can use the rewards you've earned to get them.

§ **WALGREENS REGISTER REWARDS.** The Walgreens monthly Easy Saver catalog frequently offers several items that are free after rebate. No mailing is necessary; Easy Saver rebates can be redeemed online. For more information, visit www.walgreens. com/dmi/easysaver/default.jsp.

CVS EXTRA CARE BUCKS. CVS's Extra Care Bucks are not actually rebates but coupons that print out at the bottom of your cash register tape when qualifying merchandise is purchased. Extra Care Bucks, or ECBs, as they're known in frugal circles, are then used to purchase almost any other item at CVS.

RITE AID REBATES. Rite Aid pharmacy offers a Single Check Rebate program on different products each month. Members can enter receipt information online to receive rebate checks as well as take advantage of unadvertised in-store sales. Learn more at https://riteaid.rebateplus.com.

To make the most of these programs, here's what you need to know:

- When you get to the store, scan your card at the kiosk for additional in-store coupons.
- Combine qualifying ECBs/Rebate Rewards merchandise with manufacturers' coupons and in-store coupons to maximize savings.
- Use your ECBs/Rebate Rewards to purchase sale items and combine them with coupons, too.
- CVS will honor competitors' coupons.
- Visit the Mommysavers.com "What's in Store" forum at http://mommysavers.com/boards/whats-store to get the inside scoop on what ECB and Rebate Rewards purchases are the best deals of the week. More often than not, at least a few things each week are completely free after coupons and rebates!

"I've been shopping at CVS for close to a year and a half. What works best for me is to sit down with my local ad and coupons and create a plan before I even enter the store. I look for the things I know I'll use (it isn't a deal if you don't use it) and pair coupons with sales. I use my ECBs to buy other things that earn new ECBs to keep them 'rolling' into new savings. Sometimes I even get things for free!"

—SUSANNAH FATER, LAKE IN THE HILLS, ILLINOIS

EASY REBATES

To make rebating even easier, use a website such as www. rebatetracker.com. Register for a free account and list your rebate details when you send them in. The site will remind you when your rebate is due so that you can track money earned and denied claims, and also calculate your success ratio. It's also a great source to learn about grocery rebates available at retailers near you.

GAS STATIONS/CONVENIENCE STORES

Known for convenience, they're also known for incredibly high prices on groceries. However, in certain areas convenience stores offer loss-leader-type prices on staples like milk, bread, potatoes, and bananas to get you into the store. Doing a little price research at your own store can yield some good bargains.

> *"For my family of four, it's cheaper to get our bread and bananas at the local convenience store (KwikTrip) than it is at Walmart. Kwik-Trip bananas are $0.39 a pound versus $0.69 at Walmart. I usually buy two or three pounds and the savings is anywhere from $0.60 to $0.90. With the difference, I can purchase an entire loaf of bread."*
>
> —AMY ARNDT, WASECA, MINNESOTA

ETHNIC GROCERY STORES

Ethnic foods offer terrific flavors at great prices. Most supermarkets are expanding their ethnic foods sections, which reflects the growing trend for preparing ethnic foods at home. There are some great bargains to be found in those departments, but you can also go right to the source to save even more money.

Since most ethnic markets have a small clientele and operate on word of mouth instead of having to pay for advertising, they are able to pass those savings on to their customers. Most Non-American cultures rely less on prepackaged foods and can offer flavorful food without all the additives and preservatives. Even if the prices aren't better, the quality of the food sold often is.

These are great places to take your children because it can be a field trip and shopping trip rolled up in one! They get a taste of another culture, and they also get to pick out some new foods to try, which encourages them to expand their palates.

HAVE THEM CHOOSE. Encourage your kids' sense of culinary adventure by allowing them to choose some new and different products to try at home.

EAT IN. Many ethnic markets also offer a small deli or food counter and seats for dining in. Plan a lunch outing so you can sample some of their products.

"The Polish grocery stores here have great deals on many spices and things like poppy seeds. They also have excellent baked goods, breads, sweetbreads, coffee cakes, and other pastries. You never know what surprising goodie you will find when you walk up and down the aisles! You will also discover varieties of cold cuts you never knew existed.

You can't beat the Arabic stores for the pita breads. They're good and fresh—not like the stuff at the chain grocery stores. You'll find all the typical Arabic foods like hummus, Spanish cheese, olives, as well as interesting things like rose jelly or date syrup."

—MARI WILSON, BLOOMFIELD HILLS, MICHIGAN

WAREHOUSE SHOPPING

If you're like one in three Americans, you belong to a warehouse club. Warehouse stores like Costco, BJ's, and Sam's Club can be a treasure trove of bargains if you know what to look for as well as what to avoid. Here are some tips to help you make the most of your membership.

 USE THAT PRICE BOOK! By keeping a log of prices you typically pay per ounce at the grocery store, you're armed with the information you need to make smart buying decisions anywhere you go (refer to price book information on page 19). When it comes to warehouse stores, don't look at the price per package; instead look at the price per ounce. Bring a calculator along if your warehouse store doesn't list it for you.

ONLY BUY WHAT YOU NEED. Buying in bulk is better when it comes to pinching pennies, right? Not always so. Since many consumers assume that bigger is always better, marketers use this mind-set to cash in. Some raise the price on their bigger bottles accordingly. The only way to know whether the bulk packaging will help you save is to do the math.

Bulk food sometimes can help you save, but if you don't use it all up before its expiration date, you're wasting food—and money. Only purchase perishable food items in bulk if you make a conscious effort to use up what you have or preserve it by stashing some away in the freezer for later.

Research shows that people tend to consume more when they purchase larger packages of consumer products (for example, you'll squirt out more shampoo when using a big bottle than using a small one). If you do purchase big packages of snacks and other food items, consider dividing them into smaller packages.

CHOOSE YOUR MEMBERSHIP WISELY. Take the membership fee into account when calculating how much you'll save. Consider sharing your membership or the products you buy with a friend to minimize the overhead costs of membership. One size does not fit all. When deciding which warehouse club to join, consider what you'll be using it for. Consumer Reports found Costco is superior for groceries and Sam's Club is better for small appliances and electronics.

CONSIDER COUPONS. If you're a die-hard coupon user, it can be better to stick to grocery stores. Currently BJ's, an East Coast establishment, is the only warehouse store that accepts coupons. Visit their website for additional coupons to use in-store: www.bjs.com/coupons/index.shtml.

TRY BEFORE YOU BUY. Give your store a trial run before committing to it. Most will offer one-day passes or let you look around before signing up for a full membership.

KNOW THE SAVINGS SECRETS. According to a recent CBS report, Sam's Club marks items with a "C" on the price tag if they've been cancelled or discontinued. If the item's price ends with a penny, it's been marked down. At Costco, look for an asterisk for discontinued goods, and anything that ends with $0.97 for markdowns.

STICK TO YOUR LIST. Great deals abound at warehouse stores, but temptation lies around every corner. It's not saving if you buy something you really don't need. Don't set foot inside the store unless you have a shopping list and the determination to stick to it.

GRAB A BITE TO EAT. If you head to the warehouse store mid-day on Saturdays and Sundays, you may be able to grab a quick bite at the same time, completely gratis. This is peak time for product samples and demonstrations.

THE BEST FOOD AND GROCERY BARGAINS AT WAREHOUSE CLUBS

Party foods and appetizers

Take-and-bake pizzas

Bakery birthday cakes

Dairy products like milk, cheese, and butter

Bulk baking supplies like yeast, flour, sugar, and oil

Bulk pasta and rice

Large institutional-size cans of tomato sauce, tomatoes, and other products

Cookware

DISCOUNT DEPARTMENT STORES

T.J. Maxx/Marshalls/HomeGoods

Discount department stores such as T.J. Maxx, Marshalls, and HomeGoods carry a small selection of gourmet sauces, spice blends, chocolates, salsas, jams, oils, vinegars, and other specialty food items. They typically carry premium brands you'd see at specialty shops at 20 to 60 percent off their original retail price. It's a great place to pick up items for a hostess gift or food gift basket.

"One of the easiest and most welcome gifts to give is food! T.J. Maxx and Marshalls make it super easy because of the price and variety of gourmet items. What I do is first browse their goodies and then choose an 'experience' for the recipient, building a theme around that one item. For example, gourmet shortbreads, flavored coffees, or exotic jams can be inspiration for a 'You're so sweet!' thank-you gift. Lastly, I look for a beautiful piece of bakeware or decorative serving piece in the clearance section to tie the theme together into a fabulous yet affordable gift."

—JENNIFER CAROTA, PITTSBURGH, PENNSYLVANIA,

WWW.THEGIFTTHERAPIST.COM

COMMISSARIES

Military families can take advantage of grocery bargains at their base commissary with a valid military ID. Since the commissary is set up as a benefit to military families, not a business, it sells at cost. Instead of having the loss leaders, the price benefit is everyday low prices.

PRICE MATCH. The commissary will also match competitors' prices, so don't forget your sales fliers from other stores when you go. Check out their website, www.commissaries.com, for notice on when the sales are.

ASK FOR RAIN CHECKS. If sale items are sold out at either the commissary or PX, be sure to ask for a rain check. Even with a rain check you're not obligated to buy, but you'll have the option of purchasing the item later at the sale price.

$ **DON'T FORGET YOUR COUPONS!** However, if you do, many commissaries have coupon bins for their customers to peruse. And for military families overseas, coupons may be used up to six months past their expiration date.

FOOD OUTLETS/RESTAURANT SUPPLY CHAINS

A food outlet such as a restaurant supply chain can be a good place to shop not only for food items but also for cleaning supplies and appliances as well. Visit these sites for more information:

- $ www.smartandfinal.com
- $ www.smartfoodservice.com
- $ www.gfs.com

Shop Online for Food

Most people overlook online food shopping because of the added delivery charges, but it can still be a part of a frugal routine. You'll be saving the time it takes to collect items in your cart, check out, and drive home—and, as the saying goes, time is money. Even if you only have a portion of your grocery order delivered—your nonperishables, for example—you'll be saving a huge amount of time. Additionally, you'll avoid being tempted by impulse items at the checkout counter.

Many brick-and-mortar supermarkets also allow you to place your order online and have it delivered or pick it up at the store. They include Harris Teeter, Safeway, and Vons.

AMAZON.COM

This site offers a wide selection of boxed meals, toiletries, hot drinks, cereals, and other grocery products. Most are packaged and sold in bulk and come with free shipping on a minimum order.

💲 **CLICK THE SAVE.** Click the "Sales and Special Offers" section for the best deals.

💲 **SAVE MORE.** If you're a regular customer, check out the "Subscribe and Save" option, which allows you to save an additional 15 percent on items shipped to you at regular intervals of your choice.

WEBVAN.COM/HOMEGROCER.COM
Powered by Amazon.com, it's heavy on household supplies, dried spices, and snack products. Most selections are only available in bulk.

💲 **TOP TIP.** Try viewing "top sellers" for hidden bargains.

FRESHDIRECT.COM
Currently available in the greater New York City area, it offers a variety of ready-to-eat meals as well as organics and other groceries.

💲 **FIND THE SALES.** Visit the "Our Picks" section to see which products are on sale.

MEXGROCER.COM
Offers a selection of food-related gift items as well as Mexican basics and gourmet specialties. It'll ship to any valid address within the continental United States, Alaska, Hawaii, and APO/ FPO military addresses.

$ **SAVING TIME IS SAVING MONEY.** You may not find the best bargains here, but you may discover some otherwise hard-to-find items.

NETGROCER.COM

It has over 3,500 items to choose from and ships anywhere in the United States via FedEx.

$ **KNOW YOUR PRICES.** Listed prices are sometimes higher than those at typical grocery stores.

PEAPOD.COM

This site is available in certain parts of the East Coast and in the greater Chicago area.

$ **CLICK THE "SPECIALS" TAB** for a selection of groceries up to 50 percent off or buy one, get one free.

WEGOSHOP.COM

Wegoshop.com relies on independent contractors in certain areas of the United States, Canada, and Puerto Rico to fulfill its grocery orders. Order forms are filled out online, and the customer pays a flat fee or a percentage on the grocery total.

$ **ENJOY GROCERY SHOPPING AND COMPARING PRICES?** Wegoshop.com is looking for individuals to start grocery delivery services in their area. Earn some money while you're shopping for others.

"I get a lot of my organic grocery items through Amazon.com's Subscribe and Save program, where I get 15 percent off the regular Amazon price plus free shipping. I've also set up a regular delivery schedule on products like natural cleaners, gluten-free products as well as diapers and wipes. This way, I can plan ahead with my meals and my budget. I know exactly when my items will arrive because they send an email before actually shipping the item out."

—SANDRA KNUTSON, POWAY, CALIFORNIA

The Multiple-Store Strategy

Which market has the lowest overall prices? The answer is never just one store.

COMBINE TO FIND THE BEST DEALS. Because any supermarket would go out of business if it undercut its competitors on all fronts, the answer is to use a combination strategy that includes shopping at more than just one store. Shopping multiple stores doesn't require more than one trip a week; it just means being selective about what you buy at each location and stocking up when you're there.

ALTERNATE SHOPPING TRIPS. Shop at Store A one week, purchasing the items that are the best value *there*. Shop at Store B the next week, purchasing *its* best bargains. At each store, purchase enough to last until you're there again, which may be at least a two-week supply.

💲 **DON'T WASTE GAS.** Try to avoid making too many trips to save time as well as gas.

💲 **USE YOUR PRICE BOOK.** If you've created your price book (see page 19), you'll begin to notice which stores have consistently low prices on certain favorites, and you can plan your stops accordingly.

EAT HEALTHY FOR LESS

Okay, so you're spending less on food. But is that food good for you? If not, you may end up paying more in health care and other costs down the road. Saving money doesn't have to involve shopping sales or using coupons all the time, but simply being a smart shopper.

Eating healthy on a budget requires a paradigm shift. Instead of thinking of price as the only factor guiding your purchasing decisions, you also have to consider the value of what you're getting. Sometimes the truly frugal product will cost more than a cheaper alternative, but you'll get more nutrition for your money. You also need to keep in mind that paying for empty calories or poor nutrition is never a good idea—even when the price is right.

Healthy Habits to Lighten Your Wallet—and Your Weight

Don't let money be the excuse that stands between you and a well-balanced diet. By gradually implementing the tips below, you'll be well on your way to a healthier, more frugal lifestyle. It isn't what you're spending; it's what you're eating that makes the biggest dent in your budget. Follow these tips and you'll be on your way to saving your health as well as a lot of money.

LIMIT PREPACKAGED FOODS.

- Shop the perimeter of the store and you'll avoid prepackaged foods that often contain a lot of sodium, fat, and preservatives.
- Learn to cook your favorite foods at home and you'll spend less money while eating healthier.
- If you're short on time, make double batches and freeze one to eat later.
- Slow cookers can be lifesavers. They are also great tools for creating healthy meals that don't require a lot of prep time.

USE MICHAEL POLLAN'S "GRANDMOTHER TEST." The author of *The Omnivore's Dilemma* and *In Defense of Food* recommends this: if it wouldn't be recognized as food by someone who lived a few generations ago, it probably isn't the best thing you can eat.

LIMIT PRESWEETENED FOODS. Instead of buying presweetened foods like cereals, iced teas, yogurt, etc., buy the regular version and add a teaspoon or so of sugar to taste. You'll be saving money, and chances are you won't be using nearly as much sugar as the presweetened version contains.

BUY SEASONAL PRODUCE. Buy the fruits and vegetables that are in season where you live. Length of time from harvest to consumption is shorter, which means your produce will lose fewer nutrients in transit. Local farmer's markets are great resources for healthful produce. At your local supermarkets, consider buying produce marked "locally grown."

LIMIT EMPTY CALORIES IN BEVERAGES. According to the National Soft Drink Association (NSDA), the average person consumes over 600 12-ounce soft drinks per year. Not only are sodas, sugary juices, and alcoholic drinks expensive, but they also contain a lot of empty calories that fill you up and prevent you from getting the nutrients your body needs. What's the value in that?

HOW MUCH DOES A HEALTHY DIET COST?

If you've ever wondered if your spending is on track, consider this. The USDA reports on food costs in the United States by compiling cost averages for four different plans, from cheapest to most expensive: Thrifty, Low-Cost, Moderate, and Liberal. The Thrifty Food Plan is the basis for food stamp allotments. In December 2008, food plans ranged from $120.60 per week (Thrifty) to $233.40 per week (Liberal) for a family of four with young kids. How does your spending compare?

SOURCE: WWW.CNPP.USDA.GOV/USDAFOODCOST-HOME.HTM

GO MEATLESS ONCE A WEEK. Johns Hopkins University has started a campaign to help reduce the risk of cancer, stroke, diabetes, and heart disease by going meatless just once a week. Join the challenge and you may save more than just your health. Learn more at www.meatlessmonday.com.

EAT MORE WHOLE GRAINS. Whole grains are economical and healthy. Oats, barley, wheat, and rice provide nutrition as well as dietary fiber to fill you up (see more about whole grains on page 102).

CONSUME MORE LEAN PROTEIN. Legumes like lentils and beans provide necessary protein at much more reasonable prices than meat. Plus, they contain dietary fiber and are low in fat, making them a dietary bargain. Eat meat in moderation and add more lean sources of protein to your diet.

EAT BREAKFAST. There's plenty of evidence to suggest that skipping breakfast causes you to consume more calories later on in the day. Avoid skipping breakfast and instead opt for a high-protein meal that won't leave you ravenous later on.

REDUCE OVERALL SUGAR CONSUMPTION. According to a CBS news report, the average American consumes almost 160 pounds of refined sugar each year—a 25 percent increase over the past three decades. Research suggests that sugar has an addictive property that causes subjects to crave more sugar. By limiting the amount of sugar in your diet, you'll be less hungry—thereby spending less overall on food.

Product	Price	Ounces	Price/Ounce
Nacho Cheese Doritos	$4.19	18	$0.23
100-Calorie-Pack Doritos	$2.06	3.4	$0.61
Goldfish Crackers	$1.97	6.6	$0.29
100-Calorie-Pack Goldfish Crackers	$2.69	3.75	$0.72
Lorna Doone Cookies	$3.69	10	$0.37
100-Calorie-Pack Lorna Doone Cookies	$3.29	4.44	$0.74
Chips Ahoy Cookies	$3.63	15.25	$0.24
100-Calorie-Pack Chips Ahoy Cookies	$3.29	4.86	$0.68

Alternatives to chips and cookies that typically have less fat include popcorn, pretzels, and animal crackers.

RETRAIN YOUR TASTE BUDS. It's only natural to gravitate toward favorite meals and dishes that are easy to prepare. Don't get stuck in a rut! Make it a goal to try a new recipe once a week, shopping according to what's on sale at the supermarket. Getting kids in the habit of trying a new food once a week helps get their taste buds accustomed to healthier fare, which in turn can save you money. Don't give up if your child isn't receptive to the new food at first. Research finds that children often need to be exposed to a new food anywhere from five to twenty times before it is accepted.

EAT LESS

According to the American Obesity Association, 64.5 percent of U.S. adults over age 20 are overweight. Reducing the amount of food consumed will not only lighten your budget but can also help contribute to healthy weight management. Try these tips:

 AVOID BUYING TRIGGER FOODS IN BULK. If it's there and in abundant supply, you're more likely to consume larger portions. If you want to cut back on something buy smaller containers, not larger ones.

SERVE MEALS ON A SMALLER PLATE. According to Brian Wansink, author of *Mindless Eating*, a plate is a subtle suggestion on how much to eat. We will serve 25 to 35 percent more food on a larger plate without really thinking about it.

EAT CONSCIOUSLY. Avoid distractions, such as the TV, computer, or newspaper, while eating.

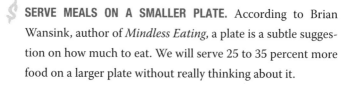

LEARN TO READ LABELS

Knowing what to look for when reading labels can help you determine if you're getting a quality product for your money. Here are some tips that can help you spot the difference between good products and those you should avoid:

- In general, the fewer ingredients the better.
- Choose products with at least 3 g of fiber per serving.

- Look for products with whole grains in the first or second position on the ingredient list. Don't be misled by terms like "wheat" or "multigrain," which don't indicate a whole-grain product.
- Avoid trans fats such as hydrogenated or partially hydrogenated oils. Keep saturated fats under 5 g per serving.
- Aim for less than 480 mg per serving of sodium.
- Avoid excess sugar in your diet. Be wary of products that list high fructose corn syrup, a cheap form of highly concentrated sugar, as one of the first ingredients.
- Watch for hidden sugars. Just because sugar isn't at the top of the list doesn't mean it's not a sugary product. Sometimes there will be two, three, or even four types of sugar on the list such as high fructose corn syrup, dextrose, corn syrup solids, brown sugar, and so on, which can disguise the true sugar content of the product.

Aisle by Aisle

A savvy shopper can save big bucks by simply looking at the products in each aisle of the grocery store in a new way. Eating a frugal, healthy diet depends on being open to new tastes and trying new things. It also helps to learn a few tricks to get the foods you already enjoy for less. Let's take a look:

Save on Produce

BUY BAGGED. Bagged potatoes, onions, and apples cost less than loose ones that are sold individually.

$ **WEIGH PRODUCE BAGS.** Even if all the produce bags say "5 pounds," it pays to weigh them when you make your selection. It's very rare that each bag weighs 5 pounds exactly. If you can get half a pound for free, why not?

$ **BUY IN SEASON AND SHOP SALES.** Let the supermarket sales determine what you buy when it comes to fresh produce. They'll often run a special on certain fruits and vegetables, and armed with your price book, you'll be equipped to spot the best buys of the week.

$ **CONSIDER FROZEN FOODS.** Frozen fruits and vegetables are a great frugal buy because they are usually more nutritious than canned, and sometimes even more nutritious than fresh produce that has been allowed to sit around. They taste pretty good if you prepare them well. Learn to make sauces and add seasonings to dress up plain frozen foods.

$ **LOOK FOR CLEARANCE PRODUCE.** Certain grocery stores will mark down produce to sell if it's nearing the end of its freshness cycle. Bananas, for instance, are often bagged and reduced for quick sale. Stocking up on these items and using them up quickly (or freezing them) is a way to get in your servings of fruit and vegetables for less. Make sure you have a plan in place to use them up.

$ **CHOOSE LOW-COST PRODUCE THAT PACKS A NUTRITIONAL PUNCH.** Potatoes of any kind are thrifty, but sweet potatoes contain more vitamins than regular red or russet potatoes. Try making sweet potato fries by coating ½-inch strips with olive oil and kosher salt, then baking them for a half hour at 425°F, turning them halfway through. Frozen green vegetables, like spinach, peas, and broccoli, are loaded with vitamins and almost always cost less than $2 per pound.

WORD TO THE WISE. Because of its high water content, iceberg lettuce has almost no nutritional value. As a rule of thumb, the darker the leaves, the more vitamins and minerals your greens will have. Instead of iceberg for salads, opt for romaine. Considering its flavor, nutritive value, and shelf life, you get a much bigger bang for your buck.

PURCHASE "REDUCED FOR QUICK SALE" FRUITS AND VEGGIES at a discount and use them in recipes that use ripe produce such as guacamole (avocado), muffins and breads (bananas), and stuffed peppers (green or red bell peppers).

"I buy any clearance produce that still looks good, making sure I use it up right away or freeze it. I will cook clearance vegetables in soups and freeze them to use later on. I'll freeze berries on cookie sheets, then put them in a freezer bag once they are individually frozen so they don't clump together. They're good in smoothies, and blueberries are easy to throw into muffins and pancakes."

—JENNIFER EVANS, THE SUGARLANDS, TEXAS

LEARN TO PRESERVE. Preserve seasonal fruits and vegetables by learning how to properly freeze them. Freeze fruits and veggies at home by placing a single layer of the food you're working with on a cookie sheet or tray and place in a chest freezer overnight. Once frozen, transfer the food from the tray to a zippered freezer bag and label with the date. Freezing with this method will prevent food from clumping together. Other methods of food preservation include canning, pickling, and dehydrating.

DID YOU KNOW? One argument people use for not eating fruits and vegetables is that they are too expensive, especially when they're fresh. Yet the U.S. Department of Agriculture found that among 154 forms of fruits and vegetables priced using ACNeilsen Homescan data, more than half were estimated to cost $0.25 or less per serving.

GROW YOUR OWN

Planting a garden is a fantastic way to get some exercise, enjoy the outdoors, and save money while you're at it. In fact, a study by the National Gardening Association determined that a $70 investment in gardening can yield up to $600 in vegetables.

If you're short on space and time, you can still grow your own produce. Even apartment and city dwellers can save money by choosing a gardening plan that works for them. Here are four easy ways to get started:

WINDOWSILL GARDENING. The most basic thing to start with is herbs, since they're ready to go from the moment you purchase a plant. Choose easy plants that can be used in a large variety of meals, such as basil, oregano, cilantro, and parsley.

LOOK FOR INEXPENSIVE GROW-YOUR-OWN HERB KITS at dollar stores, garden stores, craft stores, and even retailers like T.J. Maxx and Marshalls. They're a great way to get your feet wet with herb gardening and add some cute windowsill décor at the same time.

CONTAINER GARDENING. If you have a patio, rooftop, or deck, you can add larger outdoor containers. Since few plants can thrive completely in the shade, you'll want to make sure your area gets at least five to six hours of sunlight per day. The advantage to gardening in containers is portability. If necessary, you can move plants to achieve maximum sunlight exposure. When choosing what to grow, take into consideration your own growing conditions. Some plants do well in partial shade; others need more direct sunlight.

Five-gallon buckets work well for container gardening. Make sure you drill holes in the bottom to ensure proper drainage. Place some type of drainage component in the bottom near the holes so soil doesn't spill out. Pebbles, sand, or even newspaper works well.

SQUARE-FOOT GARDENING. This type of garden works well if you have at least a small yard but aren't quite ready for the commitment of a large garden. Section off an area in square-foot portions. For example, a 6 × 6 garden would contain 36 square feet. Each square foot houses a different plant. This is a great option if you have children. Give them a few square feet that they can water, weed, and be responsible for.

MORE GARDEN TIPS

Here are some more tips to help you get the most green out of your garden:

- **TAKE INTO CONSIDERATION WHAT YOU ENJOY EATING WHEN CHOOSING WHAT TO PLANT.** Are you a pizza lover? Consider growing your own toppings: onions, peppers, basil, and tomatoes. Love Mexican food? Try growing jalapenos and cilantro.

- **THINK ABOUT YOUR SITUATION.** Which plants will do well under your climate and sun conditions? To get expert advice according to your region, visit the National Gardening Association website: www.garden.org/regional/report.

- **CONSIDER WHAT PLANTS WILL YIELD THE BIGGEST BANG FOR YOUR BUCK.** Potatoes and other root crops, for example, are fairly inexpensive at the grocery store, so you may want to skip those in favor of something that is more cost-effective to grow yourself such as herbs, bell peppers, or tomatoes.

- **CONSIDER CREATING YOUR OWN COMPOST** to enrich soil and fertilize plants (see the section on composting on page 214).

HARVEST YOUR OWN SEEDS to use again at the end of the growing season. Select seeds from the best plants, air-dry them for a few days, and store in envelopes clearly marked with the contents.

SAVE YOUR OWN RAINWATER TO WATER PLANTS and watch your water bill go down. The easiest way to capture rainwater is by placing a large bucket or barrel at the end of a downspout. Don't buy one; build your own with instructions found online. Search "rain barrel."

GET FIVE-GALLON BUCKETS FOR CONTAINER GARDENING FREE at many restaurants just by asking.

JOIN YOUR LOCAL FREECYCLE NETWORK to take advantage of free plant starts that are given away. Be sure to boost your own Freecycle "karma" by giving your own cuttings away as well. Learn more at www.freecycle.org.

PRESERVE HERBS. Use ice cube trays to freeze herbs at the end of the growing season. Chop herbs and put in the trays with a little water and freeze. When frozen, transfer cubes to a freezer bag. You'll be able to pull them out of the freezer and use throughout the year when herbs at the grocery store are at their peak in price.

Extend the Life of Produce

Improper storage of produce can lead to vitamin and flavor loss, which is why it's so important to get the most of your investment in healthy foods. Look for easy ways to keep produce fresher longer.

ENSURE PROPER RIPENING. Some fruits and vegetables, like bananas, avocados, and peaches, haven't completely ripened when you purchase them. Leaving them on a counter is your best bet to ensure proper ripening. When they've ripened completely, transfer them to a plastic bag within your refrigerator.

STORE ROOT VEGGIES RIGHT. Root vegetables such as potatoes, onions, and sweet potatoes are best stored outside of your refrigerator.

WATCH THAT WATER. Excess moisture can encourage food spoilage, so it's a good idea to avoid washing produce until you're ready to use it.

BAGGED BARGAINS. Bagged lettuce doesn't last nearly as long as fresh lettuce, plus it's more expensive. However, for many busy families it's a great way to save time. When you do buy bagged greens, look for bags without any moisture or condensation in the bag to help extend its shelf life.

FRESH IS BEST. To extend the shelf life of lettuce and other greens, follow these steps: Remove from plastic wrap and wash.

Make sure you dry the leaves thoroughly, since excess water will cause the leaves to wilt faster. A salad spinner is the most effective way of doing this. Look for one with a plunger mechanism rather than a crank or pull-string model. Wrap leaves in paper toweling to absorb any excess moisture and insert in a plastic bag, making sure to press down to remove air bubbles before sealing. Store in the crisper drawer of your refrigerator.

WRAP IT. Wrap celery and cucumbers in aluminum foil and they'll stay fresh for weeks!

ABSORB IT. Produce-saving bags, or "green bags," are available at most grocery stores and online and claim to keep produce fresher by absorbing ethylene gas, which causes fruit and veggies to spoil. Other products include ExtraLife disks and Rubbermaid's Produce Savers. You may find that regular produce bags work just as well.

SEPARATE THEM

Ethylene, a natural gas emitted by all fruits and vegetables, ensures proper ripening. It can also lead to food spoilage. In general, fruits give off more ethylene gas, while veggies and greens are more sensitive to it. Place them in separate crisper drawers in your refrigerator to keep them fresher longer.

Ethylene-producing fruits and vegetables: apricots, avocados, bananas, cantaloupes, honeydew melons, kiwis, mangoes, nectarines, papayas, peaches, pears, plums, tomatoes

Ethylene-sensitive fruits and vegetables: apples, asparagus, broccoli, carrots, cucumbers, eggplants, green beans, lettuce and other greens, potatoes, summer squash, watermelons

SOURCE: REALSIMPLE.COM

Great Grains: Whole Grains, Pastas, and Cereals

Grains are an affordable staple of any thrifty budget. When you think of frugal cooking, who doesn't think of rice and pasta? But without variety, frugal fatigue can set in quickly. Learn to prepare a wide variety of grains, and you'll greatly expand your money-saving options. Finding some of the lesser-known grains can also be a challenge, but health food stores, food co-ops, or the organic aisles in your supermarket are good places to look.

$ **BUY IN BULK.** Keep in mind that grains are typically cheaper when purchased in bulk. Careful, not everything is!

WHOLE GRAINS

Whole grains are an important part of frugal cooking because they offer superior nutrition at reasonable prices. When combined with other amino acids, such as those found in legumes, nuts, and seeds, they create a protein, which is an economical way of getting the nutrients you need.

Plus, they contain more fiber, which can prevent heart disease, reduce cholesterol, and improve digestion. Consuming whole grains also helps you to feel full, thus preventing overeating and obesity.

BE WHOLE GRAIN SMART. Don't be confused by terms like "wheat," "organic," or "multigrain." The Whole Grains Food Council labels whole-grain foods with this logo:

THE BASIC STAMP   THE 100% STAMP

Courtesy of Oldways Preservation Trust and the Whole Grains Council; www.wholegrainscouncil.org

Here are some common whole grains and delicious cost-saving recipes to try.

Barley

Pearl barley is readily available in the supermarket and may be found next to the dried beans and lentils or in the canned soups aisle. It can occasionally be found in the bulk grains section and is almost always found at food co-ops. Most people use barley in soups and stews, but it can also be used in casseroles and as a substitute for rice in pilafs and risottos. For more uses for barley, visit www.barleyfoods.org/recipes.html.

§ **BEGINNER SUGGESTION.** Try barley beef soup instead of vegetable beef soup.

Bulgur

Bulgur is a form of wheat that has been parboiled, dried, and then ground into various textures (fine, medium, or coarse). It's common in Middle Eastern cooking and is a healthy substitute for couscous.

§ **BEGINNER SUGGESTION.** Try tabbouleh salad instead of a garden salad.

Millet

Known mainly in the Western world as a source of food for birds and livestock, millet is one of the oldest foods known to man. It is rich in B vitamins and can be purchased at health food stores. You can use it in a ton of ways, including as cereal, in muffins and breads, and in salads.

§ **BEGINNER SUGGESTION.** Try millet muffins instead of bran muffins.

Oatmeal

Oatmeal is the only whole-grain food recognized by the FDA as a way to lower cholesterol and the incidence of heart disease. Because it's loaded with fiber and antioxidants, it's one of the best frugal healthy buys on the shelves. Plus, it costs 50 to 75 percent less per serving than most cold cereals (see more about oatmeal in the cereal section, on page 115).

If eating oatmeal for breakfast doesn't appeal to you, consider the many other ways it can be prepared. It can be used as filler in meatloaf and meatballs, as a topping for desserts, as a breading or coating for fried chicken and pork, in cookies, breads, muffins, and a variety of other tasty things.

$ **SAVER SPECIAL.** Try Oatmeal is a dietary bargain any time of the year, but look for specials in January coinciding with National Oatmeal Month.

$ **BEGINNER SUGGESTION.** Try oatmeal raisin cookies instead of chocolate chip cookies

Quinoa

Quinoa, pronounced KEEN-wah, was originally cultivated in the Andes Mountains of South America. Unlike other whole grains, quinoa contains a set of essential amino acids, making it a complete protein source. When cooked it has a light, fluffy texture similar to rice or couscous.

$ **BEGINNER SUGGESTION.** Try quinoa and black beans (see the following recipe) instead of rice and beans.

Quinoa and Black Beans

1 tablespoon extra virgin olive oil

1 onion, diced

2 cloves garlic, minced

¾ cup quinoa, uncooked

1 ½ cups chicken stock

1 teaspoon cumin

¼ teaspoon chili powder

1 cup frozen corn kernels

1 15-ounce can black beans, rinsed and drained

¼ cup fresh cilantro, chopped

Sauté onion and garlic in olive oil over medium heat. Mix in quinoa and chicken broth. Add cumin and chili powder; bring to a boil. Cover, reduce heat, and simmer 20 minutes. Stir in corn, black beans, and cilantro. Heat through and serve.

Teff

Teff is a tiny, round, khaki-colored grain closely resembling millet. It's a main staple in African nations, where it's used to make injeera, a spongy bread similar to pancakes.

BEGINNER SUGGESTION. Try teff pancakes instead of using a boxed pancake mix.

Wheat

The wheat berry, which is actually the entire kernel of wheat, is something you'll see at most food co-ops, natural food stores, and in some grocery organic bulk bins. The berries are used in the same way as barley or rice is typically used in soups, salads, and pilafs. Because of their hard outer shell, they'll maintain their chewy texture without becoming mushy.

You can also use cracked wheat berries as a way to stretch meat in a meal or as a substitute for nuts.

§ **BEGINNER SUGGESTION.** Boil wheat berries for one hour to soften before using. Store in the refrigerator for two to three days or in the freezer for one month.

§ **WHEAT BERRIES CAN BE PULSED IN YOUR BLENDER** in small batches—½ cup at a time.

§ **USE AS A CEREAL.** Simply cook in your microwave, one part cracked wheat to two parts water.

For more whole-grain recipes, visit the Whole Grains Council website at www.wholegrainscouncil.org/recipes.

PERK UP YOUR PASTA

Pasta is great for many reasons: It's kid-friendly, easy to prepare, and inexpensive. However, noodles can get a little bit monotonous if eaten day in and day out. Here are some ways to perk up your pasta:

§ **BE ADVENTUROUS.** Just about every culture has its own variation on the noodle. Search the ethnic food aisles of your grocery store for Asian rice noodles, Middle Eastern couscous, or variations on European noodles.

§ **SALAD DAYS.** Step outside of your regular routine and use pasta for salads as well as main dishes. Combine with other frugal ingredients such as canned beans, homemade dressings, and seasonal vegetables.

§ **EXPERIMENTATION STATION.** Experiment with shapes, matching the sauce to the type of pasta.

- § String-like (spaghetti, angel hair)
- § Ribbon (linguine, fettuccine)
- § Tubular (penne, manicotti)
- § Stuffed (tortellini, ravioli)
- § Shaped (gemelli, orecchiete, fusilli)

In general, string shapes are good for light sauces, ribbons are good for cream sauces, and tubular pastas are best for heavy sauces. Mini pastas, such as couscous and orzo, are good for soups and salads.

§ **TRY FLAVORED PASTA.** Don't mask the flavor of the pasta by covering it up with a heavy sauce. The great thing about flavored pasta is you can go lighter on the sauce itself, which can save money. A simple olive oil and herb combination enhances the flavor instead of hiding it. Add tomato puree for a red pasta and various herbs or spinach for a green noodle.

§ **GO ONLINE FOR INSPIRATION.** Ramen noodles are well known in frugal communities as the quintessential frugal meal. In fact, there are websites devoted to the art of preparing them. To cut down on sodium, discard the flavor packet. Try www. ramenlicious.com to start.

§ **MAKE YOUR OWN PASTA.** You can experiment with making your own pasta even without special tools or equipment. No fancy pasta machines are required for making German noodles, known as Spaetzle, which can be made easily with just the pasta dough and a tin can. Other pastas can be made quickly (try the recipe below!) and cut with a knife, cookie cutter, or even biscuit molds. When stored properly in a freezer, pasta dough can be kept for up to six months. Just thaw in the refrigerator before using.

Basic Pasta Dough Recipe

2 cups semolina flour*

2 cups all-purpose flour

2 eggs, beaten

1 tablespoon extra virgin olive oil

½ teaspoon salt

Combine ingredients in mixer or food processor until smooth, adding water if necessary. Knead on floured surface until elastic. Wrap in plastic wrap and allow to rest ½ hour before use. Roll out using a rolling pin or pasta roller and shape as desired, or fill to make ravioli. You can use this basic pasta dough recipe to form just about any pasta shape.

It's important not to substitute the semolina flour, which comes from durum wheat. It creates a heavier dough with a higher gluten content, making it stronger and more pliable.

VARIETY IS THE SPICE OF PASTA. Make your own flavored pasta by adding purees to the dough. Herbs like basil or fresh spinach make a gorgeous green pasta. Roasted red peppers or tomato puree make red.

German Spaetzle

2 eggs
1½ teaspoons water
¾ cup flour
¼ teaspoon nutmeg
Pinch salt

Combine ingredients to form dough. Press dough through the holes in a colander into boiling water. The noodles will rise to the surface when they're done cooking. Serve with butter or gravy.

If making pasta from scratch isn't for you:

§ **WONTON WRAPPERS ARE A GOOD SUBSTITUTE.** Stuff them with interesting fillings such as chopped mushrooms, cream cheese, seafood, or pureed butternut squash.

§ **BUY PASTA IN BULK, WHICH CAN SAVE QUITE A BIT OF MONEY.** If you're going to stock up, go with basic shapes that can be used many different ways.

§ **MAKE YOUR OWN SAUCES INSTEAD.** Check out the Cooking Frugally and Efficiently chapter on page 185 for instructions on making flavorful sauces like alfredo, tomato, or a basic white sauce. Or, simply douse your pasta with olive oil while hot and add your choice of toppings: tomatoes, olives, mushrooms, artichokes, capers, and of course, cheese.

COUSCOUS

Couscous isn't a whole grain; it's actually a tiny pasta made from finely ground semolina flour. Because it absorbs flavor like rice, it's great to have around as a staple. Try cooking it in broths and mixing in a variety of meats, herbs, and vegetables.

BEGINNER SUGGESTION. Try couscous pilaf instead of rice pilaf.

Middle Eastern Chicken and Maftoul Couscous

Couscous:

1 carrot, diced

2 stalks celery, diced

½ onion, diced

1 clove garlic, minced

1 cup maftoul couscous (large grain)

1½ cups chicken stock

Sauté carrot, celery, onion, and garlic in olive oil until tender. Add maftoul (couscous) and sauté until brown. Add chicken stock and simmer until al dente (chewy but almost done).

Chicken:

Coat 1 bag chicken thigh and leg quarters (about 3 pounds) with:

Flour

Breadcrumbs

Dried celery

Garlic powder

Fry coated chicken in vegetable oil until brown. Place couscous in bottom of glass baking dish. Place chicken quarters on top. Bake at 350°F for ½ hour or until chicken is completely cooked.

RICE

Ah, rice. It's a bargain just about anywhere you buy it, but knowing where to shop can help you save quite a bit. Warehouse clubs typically have the best prices, but a major drawback is you have to buy it in a 25-pound bag. For other good deals, search out ethnic markets—especially Asian and Hispanic.

Store	Price	Pounds	Price Per Pound
Specialty Grocer (Whole Foods)	$3.39	2	$1.70
High-Low Supermarket (Cub Foods)	$2.88	2	$1.44
Hypermarket (Walmart Supercenter)	$1.58	2	$0.79
Discount/Limited Assortment Store (Aldi)	$1.79	3	$0.60
Warehouse Store (Sam's Club)	$11.88	25	$0.48

THE WIDE WORLD OF RICE. Learn to use different kinds of rice according to the dishes you're cooking. You'll get better results, making rice dishes more enjoyable.

Basmati—Good in pilafs, side dishes, and curries.

Jasmine—Also known as fragrant Thai rice, jasmine is good in curries and Vietnamese dishes.

Arborio—Creamy in texture, this rice is used in classic risotto dishes.

Wild—Wild rice, while not actually rice, is a healthy whole grain that's great in casseroles, soups, stuffings, and side dishes.

Brown—The whole kernel, this is the whole-grain version of white rice.

Cilantro Lime Rice

1 teaspoon olive oil

⅔ cup white basmati rice

1 tablespoon lime concentrate

1 cup water

½ teaspoon salt

2 teaspoons fresh cilantro, chopped

In a heavy saucepan, heat oil over low heat. Add rice and lime concentrate. Stir for a minute. Add water and salt. Cover and allow to simmer for about 25 minutes or until water is absorbed. Add chopped cilantro.

SAVE ON CEREAL

For many busy families on the go, cereal is an easy breakfast staple. It's also one of the easiest products to save money on. Here's how:

USE COUPONS. Cereal coupons are one of the most common coupons out there. In fact, Coupons.com reports it as their highest-volume category. If you have a favorite brand of cereal that you can find coupons for, clip or print as many coupons as possible and use them when prices hit rock bottom. Since most cereals have a long shelf life, stock up and buy several months' supply when you do.

BUY STORE BRANDS. Private-label and store-brand cereals, for the most part, taste similar or identical to more expensive brands yet cost up to 50 percent less.

SKIP THE SWEET STUFF. In general, presweetened cereals cost more per ounce than other cereals. It costs less, for example, to buy cornflakes and sprinkle a little sugar on them, or to throw some raisins on your branflakes, than to buy the presweetened versions. An even healthier option is to buy unsweetened cereal and top it with fruit.

CHECK OUT NONTRADITIONAL STORES. Nontraditional stores like Big Lots sometimes sell breakfast foods such as cereal. In fact, some offer name-brand cereals for as little as a dollar per box. Shopping there can yield big savings if you know what you're getting. In most cases the boxes are smaller than the ones you see at the store, so bring your calculator to compare the cost per ounce.

CHECK THE CLEARANCE SECTION. Look in the scratch-and-dent section of your supermarket for damaged boxes that are priced to sell. After the holidays, look for clearances on boxes with seasonal packaging.

OPT FOR OATMEAL. As we've already mentioned, oatmeal is one of the best dietary bargains in the supermarket today. It costs just pennies per serving (if you buy in bulk) and is loaded with fiber that fills you up, preventing overeating at lunch. Instead of buying the individual-size serving packets, make your own with quick oats. Not only does it costs less, but you can also control the sugar content and even add healthy mix-ins like raisins, nuts, applesauce, or fresh fruit.

GO BEYOND OATS. Besides oatmeal, other grains such as cream of wheat, grits, cracked wheat, and brown rice are great for hot cereal alternatives. Even popcorn has been known to double as a frugal breakfast alternative. According to www.popcorn.org, its use as a breakfast cereal was commonplace in Colonial America.

The Benefits of Beans and Lentils

It's no secret that meat is expensive. Even the least expensive cuts of meat typically don't go much lower than $2 per pound. Contrast that to plant-based proteins such as beans and lentils, at $1 or less per pound, and you can see that the savings is substantial, especially multiplied over time.

Not only do juicy cuts of beef and slabs of pork ring up higher at the cash register than vegetable-based proteins, but you also pay a price later on with higher health care costs. Vegetarians generally live longer than their carnivorous counterparts, and have lower incidence of heart problems and other diseases. Going vegetarian just a few days a week can help stretch your budget and improve your health at the same time.

Swearing off protein altogether isn't the answer. It's a vital part of our diets and helps keep our muscles, skin, and internal organs functioning properly. However, lean proteins such as beans and legumes cost less and offer all the nutritional benefits but virtually none of the fat and cholesterol.

Don't buy into the hype that you'll become protein-deficient if you drop meat from your diet. The truth is that unless you're taking vegetarianism to an extreme, chances are you're not going to suffer from any type of protein deficiency. Americans, on average, consume twice as much protein than they actually need. Eating too much animal protein can contribute to health problems like high cholesterol and heart disease.

HOW TO GET THE MOST OUT OF BEANS AND LENTILS

Beans have a bad reputation in the frugal community. It seems as if some people equate beans with the consummate frugal meal and perceive them as cheap and flavorless. While the frugal part of that equation may be true, they're absolutely one of the best money-saving deals going. They're also one of the longest cultivated foods on Earth, which is one reason so many countries have adopted ways of preparing them.

$ **WORLDWIDE BEANS.** Using some of this global know-how can be a fun way to add flavor (as well as a little adventure) to your diet. Here are some suggestions:

- $ Latin America: refried beans, black beans and rice, Cuban black bean soup
- $ Middle East: lentil curry, hummus, fava beans in sauce
- $ Asia: mung beans, bean sprouts
- $ Europe: Tuscan bean and vegetable soup, German sausage and bean casserole, French cassoulet, Greek fasoulada
- $ United States: baked beans, calico bean casserole, green bean casserole

---

DID YOU KNOW? Fava beans are the most common fast food in Egypt.

Beans also contain fiber and are low in fat and cholesterol, so they are a key part of a heart-healthy diet. They're also incredibly versatile, and if prepared properly, they taste like a million bucks.

Dried vs. Canned

Dried beans have an extremely long shelf life and are almost always a better deal than canned. You may look at the difference between canned beans and dried beans and think there's not much difference in price by weight. A small bag of beans may sell for $0.69, and a similar-size can of beans for $0.79. However, the dried beans will expand to three times their original size, giving you a much bigger bang for your buck.

> 💲 **BULK IT UP.** Buy dried beans in bulk to save even more.
>   1 cup dried beans = 3 cups cooked beans
>   1 pound dried beans = 6 cups cooked beans

> 💲 **SOAK UP FOR SAVINGS.** Unfortunately, in today's hurry-up society, dried beans are often overlooked because they require soaking before they're served. Soaking beans isn't at all difficult but does require a little advance planning. To make the most of your time, soak several batches for the freezer. Beans will keep well up to two months.

Before you begin soaking your beans, give them a rinse in the sink. Remove any discolored beans or little pebbles that may have ended up in the bag along with them.

Traditionally, beans are either soaked in cold water overnight, or for six to eight hours. Beans will absorb the water and expand while soaking, so be sure to add at least 2 inches of water over the level of the beans to allow for expansion. It's common practice to avoid salting them until after they've been soaked.

Forgot to soak beans overnight? No worries. They can also undergo a "quick soak" where they're placed in a pot, covered with cold water, brought to a boil for two to three minutes, then taken off the heat to sit covered for an hour. If you have a pressure cooker, you can cook them in less than thirty minutes and skip the soaking altogether.

CAN IT. If you don't have time to soak beans, you can still save by having canned beans in your pantry. They're still a wonderful bargain and are extremely convenient.

FREEZING SOAKED BEANS. If you're going to be freezing soaked beans, it is a good idea to undercook them because they'll soften even more in the freezing and thawing process. If you're using the quick-soak method, they can be frozen after they've been brought to the boiling point.

Freeze beans with their cooking liquid so they don't dry out, and be sure to allow space in your freezer bag or container to allow for expansion. Thaw them in the refrigerator before using them. Frozen beans should be consumed within a month or two of freezing. After that, their flavor and texture will be less than ideal.

BEAT THE BEANS. Don't let a little flatulence get in the way of enjoying beans. To reduce gas, make sure beans are rinsed thoroughly before and after the soaking process. For canned beans, discard the liquid and rinse well. The more you eat beans, the better your body's ability will be to process them. Slowly add more fiber to your diet little by little. Drink plenty of fluids and consider adding spices that counteract flatulence such as ginger, fennel, turmeric, coriander, and sage.

LOVE THOSE LENTILS. Lentils, which are actually little seeds, are even easier to use than dried beans because they don't require soaking. They have an earthy, nutty flavor and are great in soups and stews.

Most people realize that beans and lentils are an inexpensive source of protein, but not all beans are created equally. Knowing how much protein you're getting per serving with each variety can help you make even better decisions about what to buy.

PROTEIN IN BEANS
(cooked)

Bean (1 cup)	Protein (Grams)
Adzuki (aduki)	17
Anasazi	15
Black beans	15
Black-eyed peas	14
Cannellini (white beans)	17
Cranberry bean	17
Fava beans	13
Garbanzos (chickpeas)	15
Great northern beans	15
Green peas, whole	9
Kidney beans	15
Lentils	18
Lima beans	15
Mung beans	14
Navy beans	16
Pink beans	15
Pinto beans	14
Soybeans	29
Split peas	16

Reprinted by permission of Zel and Reuben Allen, www.vegparadise.com

Save on Meat

Meat is the main focus of most meals—and also the most expensive—so finding ways to save on meat is a key to the frugal diet.

PARE DOWN SERVING SIZES. Did you know that a healthy serving size of meat is 3 ounces, which is the same size as a deck of cards? Most Americans eat two to three times that size. It's no wonder as a nation we struggle with obesity, heart disease, and other related health problems. Instead of serving large portions of meat, serve filling accompaniments like bread, rice, and beans on the side so nobody leaves the table hungry.

LOOK FOR SUPERMARKET DISCOUNTS ON MEAT THAT IS NEARING ITS EXPIRATION DATE. Sometimes they're marked with stickers such as "Manager's Special" or "Reduced for Quick Sale," or they may simply come with a dollars-off coupon. Pay attention to what times of the day and which days of the week meats are marked down and shop then. Look for meat after major holidays like Easter, Thanksgiving, and Christmas, when excess inventory gets marked down for quick sale. As long as meat is frozen or cooked before the expiration date, it's completely safe to eat.

SHOP THE DELI COUNTER. Deli meat is much less expensive than prepackaged meats, plus there's less packaging ending up in a landfill. Most deli counters have at least one selection that's been reduced in price for the week, so buy according to what's on sale. Some deli counters will also slice meat that you buy in their meat department, such as ham—making it less expensive yet, sometimes up to $5 less per pound.

EXTEND MEATS. Texturized vegetable protein is a healthy way to extend your meats. It's used institutionally in school cafeterias as well as in some restaurants; so chances are you've eaten it already. TVP is made from soy flour that has had its oil extracted, been cooked under pressure, extruded, and dried. It comes in chunks and needs to be rehydrated before use. The resulting product is very similar in texture to meat and has a long shelf life (up to one year) if stored properly. It is an excellent source of protein and fiber, and is incredibly inexpensive when purchased in bulk. It's commonly used in chili, tacos, spaghetti sauce, and sloppy Joes.

Substituting beans for a portion of meat or replacing the meat entirely in certain dishes is another way to eat healthier while saving money (for example, kidney beans and black beans are great in tacos). Other meat extenders include bread, oatmeal, bulgur wheat, and rice.

GRIND IT YOURSELF. This one's for the hard-core frugalists. Consider grinding your own meat. If your stand mixer accepts a grinder attachment, this is an easy route to go. If you own a food processor, you can use that as well. Chop meat into 1-inch pieces and pulse about ten times until meat reaches the desired texture. Season with salt and shape into patties. Buying chuck roast or chuck steak on sale and grinding costs less—and often tastes better—than ground beef.

$ **GO BIG.** When purchasing poultry like turkey and chicken, look for the biggest bird you can get. Turkey can be used interchangeably in chicken recipes and often costs less. Because you're also paying for bones, larger birds have more meat per pound than smaller ones. If you can't eat the entire thing at once, ask your butcher to cut it in half. Most will happily oblige.

$ **BUY FAMILY PACKS.** Buy big and divide. Family packs are often more economical than purchasing pieces separately. A kitchen scale works well and is a worthwhile investment if you find yourself frequently dividing packages of ground beef into one-pound portions to freeze.

$ **SAVE THE BONES.** Don't throw the carcasses and bones away. Instead, use them to make savory broths and stocks that can be made into soups and stews. Ask your butcher if he has any bones—sometimes you can get them for free!

$ **BUY THE ENTIRE BIRD AND SAVE.** One of the best ways to save money on poultry is to purchase a whole chicken and break it down yourself. You'll get eight separate pieces—two each of the breast, thighs, wings, and legs, which can each be used in separate meals. This will save you about a dollar per pound, which can add up to big savings over time. Additionally, you'll be able to make a great chicken stock with the carcass and bones.

HOW TO CUT APART A WHOLE CHICKEN

You'll need:

- A sharp butcher's knife
- Kitchen shears
- Cutting board

Steps:

- Trim off wing tips with kitchen shears.
- Cut leg and thigh quarter away from the body.
- Cut thigh and leg apart between joint.
- Remove breast from the back, cutting down the spine.
- Pop out the keel bone (cartilage) with your fingers and separate the breasts down the middle.

If you're new to cutting a chicken apart, check out video demonstrations online to get a better idea of how to do it.

HOW TO COOK A WHOLE CHICKEN

ROASTING IN THE OVEN. If you've ever cooked a turkey for Thanksgiving, you know how easy it is. Roasting a chicken is just as simple, takes less time, and is just the right size for most families. Here's how:

Preheat oven to 350°F. Take the bird out of its bag and remove the giblets. Place on a roasting pan breast side up. Rub with olive oil and season to taste. A little garlic powder or poultry seasoning tastes great, or try some Herbes de Provence. Roast for approximately 20 to 25 minutes per pound. A meat thermometer will help indicate when you're done—target internal temperature is 165°F. Let the bird sit for 10 minutes prior to carving.

SLOW COOKER METHOD. Spray the slow cooker with a nonstick cooking spray to ease cleanup. Season the chicken to taste. There's no need to add liquid, as the chicken will cook in its own juices. Set the slow cooker on low and allow chicken to cook for 6 to 8 hours or until done. When it's finished you'll be able to easily remove the meat from the bone; plus, you'll have a nice stock left over as well.

A four- to five-pound roasting chicken feeds a family of four quite handily with leftovers for another meal. If you can't use the leftovers right away, dice the chicken, put it in zipper bags, and freeze to use later.

> *"The number one trick that I always use is to buy meat when it is reduced, especially ground beef. I will buy it in five- to six-pound packages, bring it home, unwrap it, and rewrap it in freezer paper and freeze it. Some of the quick ideas I do with such large quantities of ground beef [are to] divide it up into one-pound packages, make preshaped hamburgers, or crumble and brown some of the ground beef up so that it is all ready for whatever meal I have planned."*
>
> —AMY ARDT, WASECA, MINNESOTA

FOUR TECHNIQUES TO MAKE CHEAP CUTS OF MEAT TASTE LIKE A MILLION BUCKS

Who says melt-in-your-mouth meat has to cost a lot? Sometimes the best flavors are a result of how they're prepared, not what you spend on them. In fact, there are ways to make even the cheapest cuts of meat taste fantastic.

SLOW COOKING. Cooking over low temperatures for a long period of time will help tenderize even the toughest cuts of meat. Slow cookers are great for this technique.

SALTING. Liberally coat both sides of the meat with a high-quality salt such as kosher or sea salt. Pat in the salt a little to make it stick. Add seasoning to taste if desired, such as rosemary or garlic. Leave the salt on for about thirty minutes, but not longer than one hour. Before cooking, make sure you rinse the salt off the meat and pat dry. This will break down the proteins in the meat, improving the texture and flavor. Bring steaks to room temperature before cooking for the best results.

PRESSURE COOKING. A pressure cooker will cook tough cuts of meat in a short period of time, up to 70 percent faster than other methods, making it a great frugal option for busy families. For best results, brown meat before cooking to seal in the juices and add extra flavor. Add meat, stock, and veggies to the pot and cook according to instructions in your manual.

MARINATING. Try marinating cheap cuts of meat in an acid-based solution such as vinegar or lemon juice overnight. You can even get creative with your marinades, using acidic liquids you'd normally throw away, like pineapple juice, pickle juice, and even stale soda. The acids in the liquid will break down the tough meat fibers, making them tender and more flavorful.

TUNA: FRUGAL IMPOSTOR?

When you think of the cheapest meat option in the stores today, your mind might turn to canned tuna. However, price comparisons will show you that pound per pound, whole turkey and chicken can cost less. The comparisons below are based on the everyday non-sale price of fryer chickens and entire turkeys at a limited-assortment discount store.

Meat Price Comparisons	Cost	Ounces	Price Per Ounce
Turkey, whole	$0.79	16	$0.05
Chicken, whole	$0.99	16	$0.06
Tuna, canned	$0.59	6	$0.10

Since poultry also comes with the bones, it's only fair that the actual price of the meat itself after it's been cooked and taken off the bones be taken into consideration. A general guideline is that one pound (sixteen ounces) of whole poultry on the bone will yield eight ounces of meat off the bone. Using cooked meat only as our guide, turkey still maintains a slight price edge over tuna, but chicken is in a dead heat.

Meat Price Comparisons	Cost	Ounces	Price Per Ounce
Turkey, whole, cooked, off the bone	$0.79	8	$0.10
Chicken, whole, cooked, off the bone	$0.99	8	$0.12
Tuna, canned	$0.59	5	$0.12

Given this price information, you still have to weigh the pros and cons of each type of meat. Canned tuna's advantages are that it is cooked and ready to go, while poultry takes time to cook and to remove from the bones. Tuna also has an extremely long shelf life and can be kept up to three years under proper storage conditions. However, if you prefer the taste of poultry over tuna, realize that by buying the entire bird, you're getting a bargain. The carcass isn't a total waste, either. It can be used to create a flavorful stock that can be used in soups, casseroles, risottos, and other dishes.

Save on Dairy Products
MILK

The easiest way to find the best deals on milk is to simply shop around. Warehouse stores and discount grocers like Aldi are a good bet, but often the best prices aren't at the grocery store at all. Convenience stores running loss-leader promotions (some carry bagged milk) and drugstores such as Walgreens are also good places to look.

HEALTHIER IS CHEAPER. Shop with your health as well as your pocketbook in mind. The lower the fat content of milk, the less it usually costs. Switching to skim milk is a good idea.

PICK THE LOW-COST BRAND. Always buy the cheapest brand available. Some stores offer a discount on one-gallon jugs of milk sold in two-packs. Consider buying them to save additional money.

DON'T PAY EXTRA FOR CHOCOLATE MILK. If your kids enjoy chocolate milk, buy white milk and flavor it with inexpensive chocolate syrup. You'll spend less money overall, and can control the amount of syrup added.

KEEP IT FRESH. Since your refrigerator doors are farthest away from the cooling element, store your milk on a shelf to help keep it fresher longer. Avoid removing milk from the container in which you purchased it to store in something else, and always make sure the lid is tightly capped.

FREEZE IT. Milk can be stored in your freezer as well. Be sure to pour a little off the top to allow for expansion. This works well with low-fat milk (2 percent or lower). Be sure to thaw completely in the refrigerator and shake to redistribute the fats prior to use. Not only does freezing milk allow you to stock up when you see a good buy, but it can also help extend the time necessary between trips to the supermarket.

POWDERED MILK

Milk in its dry form, or powdered milk, typically costs less per ounce. Since fluid milk is so much heavier, it costs more to ship it. It's also great because it can be stored in the pantry for a long time. Powdered milk is a great option to use in baking and recipes such as soups and casseroles. Here are some tips to get the most satisfaction out of your powdered milk.

- **HOLD THE WATER.** If a recipe calls for cream or condensed milk, mix the powder with half of the suggested water amount.

- **OTHER TASTING TECHNIQUES.** Many families report mixing powdered milk with "regular" milk to stretch their budgets. It does taste different from "regular" milk, so it may take a while to get used to. Try adding a drop or two of vanilla to improve the taste. Try chilling it overnight to yield the best taste results.

- **POWDERED MAGIC.** Powdered milk can also be used to create instant hot chocolate. Simply combine equal parts cocoa powder, dry milk, and sugar. Add hot water and you've got a rich, hot drink.

EGGS

Eggs are one of the best values when it comes to protein. Nutritionally speaking, you get a bigger bang for your buck with eggs than with milk, cheese, or meat.

$ **BUYING EGGS IN BULK** is generally a good idea. Some stores sell them in flats; other stores will offer cartons with eighteen instead of twelve eggs.

$ **ALWAYS COMPUTE THE PRICE PER EGG,** just to make sure you're getting the best deal possible. The United Egg Producers (UEP) classifies eggs according to weight: jumbo (30 ounces per dozen), extra large (27 ounces), large (24 ounces), medium (21 ounces), small (18 ounces), and peewee (15 ounces). Medium eggs are typically a better deal than large or jumbo eggs. According to *BH&G Good Food on a Budget*, "If the price difference between medium and large eggs is less than $0.07, the larger sized eggs are a better buy than the smaller sized eggs."

CHEESE AND YOGURT

$ **SHRED IT YOURSELF.** You can save money by buying block cheese and shredding it at home. However, since grocery stores often run sales on preshredded cheese and coupons are often readily available, it pays to always compare the price per ounce.

$ **KEEP IT FRESH.** If you do buy a big block of cheese, consider how long it will last and freeze what you can't use up while fresh. In general, most hard aged cheeses like Parmesan, Swiss, and cheddar last longer than soft cheeses. Keep the remaining cheese fresh by storing in an airtight container or wrapping it with a paper towel that has been moistened slightly with white vinegar.

TRIM MOLDY CHEESE. If a bit of mold appears on your block of hard cheese, don't throw it away. Instead, cut off the spot and one inch below and around it. Don't try this with soft cheeses like ricotta, Camembert, and feta.

FREEZE IT. Extend the life of your block cheese by vacuum-sealing it and storing it in the freezer. Grated cheese also does very well in the freezer and takes virtually no time at all to thaw.

GO UPSIDE DOWN. Some people claim that storing your container of cottage cheese upside down will extend its shelf life.

BUY BULK CONTAINERS. Yogurt can be expensive, especially if you buy it in individual packages or kid-centric packaging like tubes and so on. Consider buying the big containers of plain yogurt and adding your own flavorings or mix-ins such as strawberry jam, granola, or fresh fruit.

DO IT YOURSELF. Making your own yogurt is another option and a way to use up milk nearing its expiration date (see page 191).

Beverages

If you want to trim the cost of your grocery budget quickly, consider reducing (or giving up) consumption of all beverages other than water, milk, and high-quality fruit juices.

WATER

Opt for water, which is good for you and practically free. Getting your daily requirement of H_2O has been linked to several added health benefits:

- Weight loss
- Fewer headaches
- Improved complexion
- Better digestion
- Increased energy

TAP IS BEST. Think bottled water is safer than tap? Think again. Not only does the Environmental Protection Agency (EPA) tightly regulate our tap water supply, but many communities have also opted to include fluoride in their water, giving tap an advantage over bottled. Plus, by avoiding all those plastic bottles, you're being kind to the environment as well as your pocketbook.

BRING YOUR OWN BOTTLE. To make water easy, convenient, and portable, fill up a water bottle and keep it with you at all times.

KEEP IT CHILLY. Before you go to bed, fill your water bottles halfway full and stick them in the freezer. In the morning, top off with water and it will remain cold for hours.

TREAT YOURSELF. Adding a little lemon or lime is a refreshing treat that may keep you motivated to stick with it. Or keep a few fresh mint leaves in a pitcher of water overnight to add a subtle yet fresh taste.

SODA, JUICES, AND OTHER SWEETENED DRINKS

There are several ways to conserve cash on these beverages:

SODA STOCKPILING. When you do purchase soda, stock up when your favorite brand is on sale.

BE BRAND-FLEXIBLE. Some soda brands tend to go on sale more often than others. This is one category where you can really save money by giving up your brand loyalty.

STORE-BRAND SAVINGS. Additionally, you can save even more by purchasing store-brand products. Most come with a money-back guarantee. If you don't like the taste, you can return it for a full refund.

BOTTLE SERVICE. Two-liter bottles (or even three-liter bottles, sold at some dollar stores) are an economical choice as long as you can consume it before it goes flat and it doesn't encourage you to drink more than you usually would have.

READ THE FINE PRINT. You may think you're doing yourself a favor by loading up on juices, but read the labels carefully. Some are merely made of high-fructose corn syrup, artificial flavorings, and very little actual juice. Labels like "fruit drink," "fruit flavored," "fruit beverage," or "fruit cocktail" all are indications that you're getting something less than 100 percent fruit.

§ **GO STRAIGHT FOR THE SOURCE.** Don't buy the juice! Eating the fruit itself instead of drinking juice will yield all the same nutrients as well as fill you up because of the added fiber content.

§ **100 PERCENT OR NOTHING.** If you do enjoy juice, 100 percent orange juice from concentrate is a healthy yet economical choice.

§ **SIZE-WISE.** Portion control is another key. A normal serving of juice is six to eight ounces for an adult, four to six ounces for a child.

Lemonade

Experiment with making lemonade or limeade at home using simple syrup. Here's how:

- 1 cup sugar
- 1 cup water
- 1 cup lemon or lime juice
- 3 to 4 cups cold water

Boil sugar and water to create a simple syrup. Stir until sugar is completely dissolved. Add juice and cold water.

TIPS TO KICK THE SODA HABIT

Since soda has no real nutritive value, the best way to save is to kick the habit altogether. Since that's usually easier said than done, here are some suggestions:

- **MAKE IT HARD FOR YOURSELF TO CHEAT.** Remove temptation from your house entirely by getting rid of your soda supply.
- **WHEN YOU GET THE URGE FOR SODA, GRAB A WATER BOTTLE INSTEAD.** It's healthier and does a better job of quenching your thirst. Add some ice, a twist of lemon or some fresh mint from your garden and you'll really feel like you're living large.
- **QUIT COLD TURKEY.** Give yourself an inch, and you're likely to take a mile. Don't be afraid of caffeine withdrawal. If you need a little boost, try a cup of coffee or tea instead.
- **COMMIT TO TWENTY-ONE DAYS.** Research shows that a behavior takes at least three weeks to become habit. At the very least, commit to give up soda for twenty-one days and reevaluate then.
- **REWARD YOURSELF WITH A SMALL TREAT** for making it the full twenty-one days. Just don't reward yourself with a soda!

"I figure that I am easily saving about $25+/week with cutting out my soda intake. It's not only the money from the actual sodas but from all the times I pass on the meals and snacks that go with them. Now I'm less jittery, I sleep better at night, and I've even lost 12 pounds!"

—JODIE RADAKOVITZ, PENRYN, CALIFORNIA

COFFEE ON THE CHEAP

It's no big surprise that a good cup of coffee doesn't have to be expensive. But did you know the equipment you use (a grinder and coffeemaker) can have a bigger impact on flavor than the coffee itself?

RATION OUT THE GOOD STUFF. Use a mixture of premium coffee and regular coffee for great taste without the expense. Sometimes it only takes about ¼ premium to ¾ regular ratio to improve the flavor of less expensive coffees.

PREMIUM SALES. Look for coffee to go on sale right after Christmas. You can often find premium beans in holiday blends like gingerbread spice, cinnamon, and peppermint stick for 75 percent off.

SECONDHAND MACHINES. Look for an old percolator coffee-maker at thrift stores. Percolators use less coffee than drip machines and don't require filters.

FILTER SAVINGS. If you run out of coffee filters, use a paper towel as a substitute until you can get to the store. To really stretch your dollar, try reusing disposable coffee filters two or three times before throwing away. Or invest in a reusable filter.

DON'T BE WASTEFUL. Don't make more than you can drink. If you do end up with extra, put it in a thermos to enjoy later.

GET THE MOST FOR YOUR MONEY BY BREWING THE PERFECT CUP OF COFFEE.
- Use water brought to room temperature before brewing.
- Use filtered tap water.
- Make sure your equipment is clean (see page 182).
- Use beans and grind them at home. A coffee grinder costs less than $20 and is a good investment for java lovers.

CREATE YOUR OWN SPECIALTY COFFEE DRINKS. Since It's reported that 63 percent of coffee drinkers occasionally consume specialty coffee drinks, learning how to make them at home can help provide that gourmet experience without the inflated price tag.

- Sprinkle cinnamon or drizzle a tablespoon of vanilla ice cream on top of the coffee grounds before brewing.
- Add a few tablespoons of hot chocolate to your cup for a mocha drink.
- Add pure extracts (almond, amaretto, vanilla, etc.) to the grounds before brewing coffee. Only a few drops are necessary—about ¼ teaspoon for half a pot and ½ teaspoon for a whole pot.

Café Mocha

3 cups milk

12 ounces evaporated milk

⅓ cup chocolate syrup

1 tablespoon instant coffee granules

1½ cups frozen whipped topping, thawed

Combine first four ingredients in a 2-quart microwave bowl. Cover with plastic wrap, folding back the edge of wrap to let steam out. Microwave on medium power for about 4 to 5 minutes until steaming, stirring as soon as it comes out. To serve, pour into five mugs, Top with whipped topping and sprinkle with cinnamon if desired.

Iced Coffee

Brew a 10- to 12-cup pot of coffee your usual way, doubling the amount of coffee that you generally use (decaf or regular). Add one

14-ounce can of sweetened condensed milk to the hot coffee. Refrigerate until cold. Add pure vanilla, to taste, to the coffee just before serving. Pour over a tall glass of ice.

BEER AND WINE

Even in tough economic times, beer and wine consumption usually holds steady. It's where beer and wine are purchased that changes. Because a bottle of wine at home can cost the same as a single glass at an elegant restaurant, more and more people buy alcohol for home consumption to save money. Knowing a few tricks can help you find some hidden bargains and save even more.

LOVE THE LOW-COST. Find a cheap brand of beer you enjoy.

PRICE CLUBS. Look for beer bargains at warehouse stores.

CANS ARE CHEAPER. Beer in cans typically costs less than beer in bottles.

BREW YOUR OWN BEER. Over time, home brewing can help save money and become a fun hobby.

LOOK FOR LESSER-KNOWN WINES. Check out wines grown domestically or from lesser-known regions such as Chile or Argentina.

GET TO KNOW YOUR TASTE PREFERENCES and ask for recommendations based on them.

CHECK OUT BOUTIQUE WINERIES. For a special wine, shop for low-cost varieties at "boutique" wineries.

 LOOK FOR WINE BARGAINS IN OCTOBER, when wineries release new vintages.

 ABOVE ALL, ENJOY ALCOHOL IN MODERATION. Too much is harmful for more than just your budget.

YOUR SAVINGS CAN HELP OTHERS: Sometimes little things can help others in a big way. The tab of a standard soda or aluminum can is made of high-grade aluminum that can be recycled. Pull them off and collect them to give as a donation to local civic organizations, Cub Scout packs, hospitals, or schools.

Nationally, the Ronald McDonald House Charities have collected over $4 million in pop tab donations to date. Donations are collected at McDonald's restaurants. For more information on how to get involved, visit the website http://rmhc.org.

Buying Organic: What Does USDA Certified Organic Really Mean?

The USDA regulates organic food production in the United States. If buying organic is important to you, make sure you're really getting what you're paying for. Anything bearing the certified "USDA Organic" label means that:

- Farms must use natural means of fertilizing crops.
- Farms must be free of synthetic chemicals for at least three years before a certified organic crop can be grown.
- Food has not been genetically engineered (GE) in any way.
- No growth hormones have been used.
- Eggs, meat, and dairy products must come from animals that are fed with 100 percent organic feed.

Only products that have been made entirely with certified organic ingredients can be labeled 100 percent organic. Products with at least 95 percent organic ingredients can still use the label "organic" and bear the USDA seal. Organic produce SKUs always start with the number 9.

PRIORITIZE WITH THE ORGANIC "DIRTY DOZEN"

Organic fruits and vegetables are grown with less pesticide and synthetic fertilizer but can cost twice as much as conventional produce. The Environmental Working Group (EWG), a research and advocacy organization based in Washington, D.C., puts out a "dirty dozen" list of fruits and vegetables that have the highest levels of pesticide residue left over after washing. If you have to make a choice, consider spending your organic food budget on these:

- Apples
- Cherries
- Grapes, imported (Chile)
- Nectarines
- Peaches
- Pears
- Raspberries
- Strawberries
- Bell peppers
- Celery
- Potatoes
- Spinach

In certain cases you can get by with conventional produce where the peel is less permeable and less pesticide is used. These are good options to save your money and opt for the nonorganic version:

- Bananas
- Kiwi
- Mangos
- Papaya
- Pineapples
- Asparagus
- Avocado
- Broccoli
- Cauliflower
- Corn
- Onions
- Peas

TIPS TO PROTECT YOURSELF FROM PESTICIDES

If the main reason you're choosing expensive organic produce is to limit your family's contact with pesticides, there are still some things you can do with nonorganic foods to help reduce your exposure (and reduce your cash outlay).

EAT A WIDE VARIETY of fruits and vegetables to limit your exposure to one type of pesticide.

WAIT UNTIL YOU'RE READY to eat your fruits and vegetables to clean them, which will prolong their shelf life. Immerse in cold water and scrub gently with a brush.

CHEAP CLEANER. There's no need to purchase expensive produce cleaner. Cold water works just fine. Be sure to wash your hands before preparing any type of food.

§ **BUYER BEWARE.** Purchase produce grown in the United States and regulated by the USDA. Foods from other countries don't abide by the same stringent guidelines and may have been grown with harsher fertilizers and pesticides.

§ **CUT OUT DAMAGED OR BLEMISHED PARTS**, where bacteria can thrive.

§ **CLEAN YOUR GREENS.** When it comes to leafy greens like lettuce and cabbage, peel off and discard the outer layer, which contains the bulk of the pesticide residue.

§ **CONSIDER STORE BRANDS.** Store brands and private labels are getting in on the act of providing organics to consumers, and they're able to do so for less. According to a report published by J.D. Power and Associates, consumer sentiment toward private-label organic products is positive and associated with quality on par with name brands. Notable private labels in the survey included Safeway, Trader Joe's, and Whole Foods.

Product	Price	Ounces	Price/Ounce
Store Brand Organic Apple Juice	$3.50	64	$0.06
RW Knudsen Organic Apple Juice	$4.04	32	$0.13
Store Brand Organic Peanut Butter	$3.09	18	$0.17
Arrowhead Mills Organic Peanut Butter	$6.33	16	$0.40
Store Brand Organic Ketchup	$3.23	20	$0.16

Product	Price	Ounces	Price/Ounce
Heinz Organic Ketchup	$2.88	15	$0.19
Store Brand Organic Macaroni and Cheese	$1.50	6	$0.25
Annie's Organic Macaroni and Cheese	$2.04	6	$0.34
Store Brand Organic Whole Wheat Penne	$1.69	12	$0.14
Hodgson Mill Organic Whole Wheat Penne	$2.19	12	$0.18

SHOP AROUND. Keep a log of organic prices in your price book to keep tabs on which stores offer the best prices. Stores that specialize in organic foods, like Trader Joe's and Whole Foods, have store brands that are often less expensive than supermarket organics. Take advantage of coupons and sales and stock up.

"I follow lists like the 'dirty dozen' when deciding which products to buy. I purchase organic apples, which usually top the list, but bananas, with their outer skin that you peel, I will buy in the nonorganic form. During the summer months I raise a garden and can or freeze much of my produce. I also buy locally from farmers, though not certified organic, that I know and trust their product."
—MELINDA SUE BRINKMAN, BONNERS FERRY, IDAHO

Going Green (for Less Green)

These days everyone wants to do the right thing for our environment. However, looking at the prices of organic groceries can make the most well-intentioned shopper abandon her eco-friendly ways at the checkout lane. You don't have to choose between your budget and the environment. Be kind to both!

- **BUY IN BULK (IF YOU'LL USE IT ALL).** By buying in bulk you're getting more product for the amount of packaging needed. You also typically get more for your money. Make sure you properly store things when you get home so they stay fresh. Buying too much product and not using it is counterproductive.

- **PASS ON THE PLASTIC.** When asked "Paper or plastic?" at the checkout lane, say neither. Most grocers today either sell reusable grocery bags or offer incentives for bringing your own bags. Pass on the plastic bags in the produce aisle, too. You really don't need them.

- **DITCH THE DISPOSABLES.** Use cloth instead of paper. I'm not just talking diapers, but any paper product that may be on your list: paper towels, paper plates, plastic dinnerware, etc. If you must purchase paper products, look for those made out of recycled paper. Skip the aluminum and plastic wraps and instead use reusable containers to store food. If you buy paper coffee filters, invest in a reusable one made of fabric. The fabric helps to absorb acids in the coffee, resulting in a better coffee.

Once you've made the initial investment, reusable products will pay for themselves over and over again.

$ **ABOUT THOSE OTHER DISPOSABLES....** Eat up those leftovers! Although wasted food is biodegradable, it can take up landfill space. If you must dispose of food, consider composting it. You're composting when you allow organic things (such as food scraps) to decompose naturally, resulting in a rich soil. Read how to create your own composting bins on page 214.

$ **BUY LOCAL.** Local farmer's markets, CSAs, food co-ops, and buying clubs are a great source of affordable produce. (See page 70 for more information).

$ **EAT LESS MEAT.** The United Nations Food & Agriculture Organization reports that livestock production is responsible for more climate change gases than all the motor vehicles in the world. In fact, beef production emits thirteen times the greenhouse gas as poultry production, and fifty-seven times as much as potato production.

No, you don't have to become a vegetarian—simply reducing the amount of red meat you consume can help greatly. Plus, replacing the meat in your diet with more sources of lean and vegetable-based protein doesn't only help cut expenses—it is also a part of a healthier diet. Try one or two meatless meals per week. You can also use meat as an ingredient in a pasta sauce instead of a main course without feeling deprived.

STOCKING YOUR KITCHEN

A well-stocked kitchen and pantry are musts for any budget-savvy family. It ensures you'll always have the supplies you need at your fingertips to create inexpensive, healthy meals.

Stockpiling

A price book is the best tool in your arsenal to save money. If you haven't started a price book already, turn to page 19 to find out how. You'll be using it to spot the best deals at the grocery store so that when prices hit rock bottom, you'll be able to stock up. This is a process known in frugal communities as stockpiling. It can be a lot of work, and it's not necessary to stockpile in order to take advantage of many of the tips in this book, but if you're trying to save money on food, you need to know about it.

Being a proactive shopper is the foundation for any stockpiling strategy. Instead of being a reactive shopper and buying food items when you run out of them, a stockpiler buys them when the prices are their lowest and stores them in a pantry or freezer. In order to save the most, choose to stockpile the items your family eats regularly that have the biggest difference between regular and sale prices. This smart shopper goes beyond a normal purchase at the grocery store and buys enough of the product to last until the item goes on sale again.

TOP TEN FOODS TO STOCKPILE*

Cereal

Beef

Chicken

Canned/frozen fruit

Canned/frozen vegetables

Canned tomatoes/spaghetti sauce

Cheese

Pasta

Flour/sugar/baking supplies

Bread

*Chosen by the members of the Mommysavers.com forums

In general, nonperishables work best for stockpiling: canned goods, toiletries, and dry goods such as pasta and rice. Keep like items grouped together: soups in one area, veggies in another, pastas in another, and so on. If you have a freezer, you can also include things like meat, vegetables, bread, cheese, and certain fruits (see page 220 for tips on how to store in the freezer). Think of your stockpile as a miniature supermarket. After you've successfully built up your stockpile, you will be able to shop your pantry instead of going to the store.

STOCKPILING TIPS

DON'T TRY TO BUILD YOUR STOCKPILE ALL AT ONCE. Instead, allocate a certain amount of your grocery budget each week to purchase the best deals. Focus on the bargains that yield the most overall savings and add them to your pantry little by little.

CREATE A TOP TEN. Write down a list of the ten meals you eat most frequently and the ingredients necessary to prepare them. Then you can easily see what you eat on a regular basis—and what you should be stockpiling. It's not a bargain at any price if it doesn't appeal to your family and ends up sitting on your pantry shelf.

AVOID "FRUGAL FATIGUE." Learn new ways to prepare commonly stockpiled foods to avoid this common problem. For example, if you're only using jarred marinara sauce for spaghetti, shake things up a bit by making meatball sandwiches or manicotti instead.

DON'T OVERBUY. Know how much your family really needs and purchase accordingly. Otherwise, you're wasting valuable storage space within your home.

That case of baby cereal may have been a bargain, but will your child still be eating it when he's five? A general rule of thumb for stockpiling is to buy what your family uses in two or three months. For example, if you go through one box of dry cereal a week, your stockpile may include eight to twelve boxes. If your family eats spaghetti every other week, you may want to include four to six jars of sauce in your pantry. Most times you'll see grocery prices drop again within that time frame, so you'll be able to replenish your supply when you start to run low.

WHEN TO BUY

$ **WATCH THE CALENDAR!** Holidays, national food holidays, and celebrations (see below) as well as other seasonal events all cause supermarkets to run promotions, resulting in good discounts.

January

National Diet Foods Month

National Hot Tea Month

National Wheat Bread and Bread Machine Baking Month

National Soup Month

National Fiber Focus Month

Super Bowl: Snacks like chips, salsa, pretzels, and soda

HIT THE SUPERMARKET ON DECEMBER 26

Everyone raves about after-Christmas sales, but they often forget to shop their grocery stores.

- **CHECK THE SEASONAL AISLE OF YOUR SUPERMARKET** for bargains on kids' cereals, cookies, and snacks that have holiday packaging. Your children won't know the difference!

- **FRUIT BASKETS AND CHEESE AND MEAT TRAYS.** These and other prepackaged items are great to buy if you can eat them up (or freeze certain components) right away. Look for them right after Christmas at big-box retailers and specialty shops.
- **SHOP FOR CANDY AND BAKING ITEMS AS WELL**—just be sure to pay attention to expiration dates. Red and green M&M's are great to buy; save the red ones for Valentine's Day and the green ones for St. Patrick's Day (your kids will have fun sorting them!).

February
  National Canned Food Month
  National Snack Food Month
  Valentines' Day: Candy

March
  National Frozen Foods Month
  National Flour Month
  St. Patrick's Day: Corned beef, cabbage, potatoes, carrots

April
  National Pecan Month
  National Garden Month
  National Soy Foods Month
  Easter: Ham, eggs, lamb, potatoes, etc.
  Kosher foods

May

National Egg Month

National Salad Month

National Barbecue Month

National Hamburger Month

Cinco de Mayo: Tacos, enchiladas, salsa, sour cream, etc.

Memorial Day: Buns, hot dogs, meats for grilling, ketchup, mustard, pickle relish, and sodas as well as paper goods like napkins and paper plates

June

National Dairy Month

National Iced Tea Month

July

National Picnic Month

National Hot Dog Month

National Ice Cream Month

National Baked Bean Month

August

National Watermelon Month

National Sandwich Month

Back to school: Lunch box items, drink boxes, snacks, etc.

September

National Rice Month

National Potato Month

National Honey Month

National Chicken Month

National Breakfast Month

National Mushroom Month

October

National Dessert Month

National Cookie Month

National Pasta Month: Sauces, pasta, as well as accompaniments like breadsticks and Parmesan cheese

National Pork Month: Sausage, ham, bacon

National Seafood Month: Fish, shrimp, crab, lobster, tuna

Halloween: Bagged candy

November

Leftover candy from Halloween (freeze to use in holiday baking)

Thanksgiving: Turkey, stuffing, sweet potatoes, frozen pies, cranberries, green beans, Jell-O, etc.

Baking supplies: Sugar, flour, frosting, nuts, etc.

December

Baking supplies: Sugar, flour, frosting, nuts, etc.

Holiday meats: Turkey, ham, beef brisket

SEASONAL PRODUCE

Fruits and vegetables are best when purchased in season, not just for price but for peak flavor as well. Stockpile them by preserving through freezing or home canning (see page 220 for more information).

> **PAY ATTENTION.** If you're not sure which fruits or vegetables are in season, check out store cues such as price and supply. If watermelon is in season, chances are huge containers will be available at your store at a good price. If they're hard to find within the store and expensive, they're not likely in season. A listing of seasonal produce can be found at www.fruitsandveggiesmorematters.org.

Building Your Pantry

Keeping a well-stocked pantry will allow you to have the ingredients on hand to create frugal meals without having to run to the store (saving time and gas!). Create a list of foods to have on hand all the time based on your family's favorite meals and taste. Use your price book spreadsheet, if you've created one, to make it even easier. The following basics will allow you to create hundreds of different meals without making trips to the store for additional ingredients. They're basic building blocks of any frugal pantry.

REFRIGERATOR BASICS

- Milk
- Butter, margarine
- Eggs
- Assorted cheeses
- Sour cream
- Cream cheese
- Mayonnaise
- Onions

- Garlic
- Celery
- Carrots
- Parsley
- Bouillon or powdered soup base (beef and chicken)
- Ketchup
- Mustard
- Horseradish
- Lemon juice
- Worcestershire sauce
- Soy sauce
- Maple syrup

FREEZER BASICS

Stockpiled sale meats: ground beef, chicken, bacon, pork, etc.

PANTRY BASICS

- Sugar
- Honey, molasses, corn syrup
- Flours (whole wheat, white, self-rising)
- Grains (rice, bulgur, oatmeal)
- Pasta (including couscous)
- Dried beans (kidney, black, chickpeas, white)
- Dried lentils
- Brown sugar
- Baking powder
- Baking soda
- Powdered milk
- Cornstarch
- Cornmeal
- Extra virgin olive oil
- Vegetable oil
- Vegetable spray
- Vinegars (white vinegar, red wine vinegar, apple cider vinegar)
- Canned tomatoes, diced
- Canned tomato sauce and paste
- Canned seafood (clams, crabmeat, tuna)
- Oatmeal or dry cereal
- Peanut butter
- Popcorn

DRIED HERBS AND SPICES

- Basil
- Oregano
- Dill
- Cumin
- Chili powder

- Paprika
- Mustard, ground
- Garlic powder

PRODUCE BASICS

Your produce basics will revolve around buying seasonally and according to what's on sale.

Organizing Your Pantry

How many times have you gone to the store to buy something, only to find out later that it was already sitting on your pantry shelves? A well-organized pantry will help prevent unnecessary trips to the store to buy something you may already have on hand.

 ALLOW FOR EASY REACH. Put the products you use most often on the easiest shelves to reach; the things you use less frequently can go up higher.

STORE HEAVY ITEMS LOW. Store soda cases, large bags, and other heavy items down low to avoid dropping them from overhead.

FACE "SPINES" OUTWARD. Arrange boxes as you would on a bookshelf, with the "spine" facing outward.

DONATE. Regularly donate items you don't use to a local food pantry. If you can't remember when or why you purchased it, give it away. Your loss can be someone else's gain.

MINIMIZE CONTAINER CLUTTER. If a box or bag is only half full, transfer it to a smaller container.

CONSIDER ALTERNATIVE STORAGE. If you are an apartment dweller or have limited space, think about places such as closets, bookcases (cover with an attractive curtain), or under the bed.

GROUP SIMILAR ITEMS TOGETHER. Store canned fruits, vegetables, soups, and other similar foods together on shelves.

CHOOSE SQUARE EDGES. If you use storage containers, opt for square or rectangular edges to maximize your use of space.

ALLOW FOR EASY SNACKING. Having snacks in one handy location will help prevent kids from shuffling through your organized shelves.

STORE PACKETS IN BOXES. This way you can flip through them quickly.

USE LAZY SUSANS. An easy storage option for spices or cans.

§ **LABEL NON-TRANSPARENT CANISTERS** and containers so you know what's inside.

§ **USE AIRTIGHT CONTAINERS.** Store flour, sugar, rice, beans, and lentils in airtight containers after they've been opened.

§ **USE SECONDARY STORAGE.** If you're a stockpiler, consider setting up an additional pantry for overflow in your basement or garage.

§ **MAKE SURE YOUR PANTRY IS WELL LIT.** For an inexpensive alternative to hard-wired lighting, consider a touch-light for about $10.

§ **ELEVATE ITEMS.** So they're easily visible. Or create shelves inexpensively using bricks and lightweight plywood.

SMALL SPACE STORAGE

If you don't have a large pantry, you'll need to find space for all your goods. Shelves in a basement work well. You may also want to consider moving some things out of your kitchen cupboards, such as appliances and cookware you don't use very often, to make room for your stockpile.

§ **CLEAR OVER-THE-DOOR SHOE ORGANIZERS** work well for storing spice packets, mixes, and other small items.

$ **UNDER THE BED.** If you have a dust ruffle, store canned goods under the bed and out of sight.

$ **THINK OUTSIDE THE KITCHEN.** Unused space in armoires, dressers, and coat closets can hold portions of your stockpile.

KEEP AN INVENTORY

An organized pantry needs regular checkups, and keeping an inventory is a good way to do that. With an inventory, you have the entire contents of your pantry at a glance without searching for anything, which also helps to keep it neat and tidy.

Keeping an inventory of your pantry is easier than it sounds.

$ **POST AN INVENTORY OF ITEMS** near your pantry and cross things off as you remove them. Add new things to your list after each trip to the store.

$ **CREATE A SPOT FOR FAMILY MEMBERS TO ADD ITEMS TO THE PANTRY "WISH" LIST.** Keep a running spreadsheet on your computer to make updates even easier, and post it on a small bulletin board inside the pantry door. You can even upload your pantry spreadsheet to your Palm, BlackBerry, or other Smartphone so it's easily accessible to you when you're at the store.

$ **USE THE OLDEST ITEMS FIRST.** This ensures that foods won't pass their expiration dates. When you add new items to the shelf, add them to the back instead of the front. If you don't follow this practice, be sure to "rotate" the food on the shelves periodically.

§ **REFLECT ON WHAT'S WORKING.** If you find that you're throwing foods away because they've passed their expiration date, buy a smaller box or container next time.

HOW LONG WILL THEY LAST?

BAKING SODA AND POWDER

Up to six months. Moisture can shorten its shelf life, so store in a clean, dry container.

DRIED BEANS AND LENTILS

Up to two years if stored in an airtight container.

OILS

About six months if opened and about one year if unopened. Oil will begin to develop a rancid smell, so if in doubt, take a sniff.

FLOUR

Use within one year of purchase. Whole wheat flour doesn't last as long and should be consumed within six months. Once opened, transfer your flour into an airtight container and store in a cool, dark place to extend its shelf life.

HONEY

Store at room temperature. Although honey lasts indefinitely, it can sometimes crystallize. No worries, simply heat up crystallized honey by soaking the container in a bowl of warm water.

SAUCES

Tomato-based sauces like spaghetti and pizza sauce should be used up within a week of opening them. If you don't think you can use the remainder within that time frame, freeze to use later on.

SUGARS

Brown sugar will last up to six months. Soften rock-hard brown sugar by adding a few drops of water and microwaving on medium and checking every thirty seconds. White sugar will last up to two years in an airtight container.

SHORTENING

Solid shortening will last a long time if unopened. Once opened, use within a year.

VINEGARS

One year opened; two years unopened. White vinegar, because of its acidic nature, will keep indefinitely.

CANNED GOODS

There is a public misconception that the dates on the cartons, boxes, and cans are expiration dates, when in fact they are usually "sell-by" dates that have some cushion or leeway on the back end for safe usage after the date has passed. If in doubt about food storage times, call the phone number on the can or visit the manufacturer's website for more information.

DAIRY PRODUCTS

With milk and dairy, you generally have up to seven days after the sell-by date to use it up, as long as it has been stored properly. Use your nose as your guide. Sometimes milk or other dairy products can smell a bit "off" even before their sell-by date.

EGGS

Use the float test to check eggs for freshness. Drop your egg in water and see if it floats. The best result is to have your egg sink to the bottom and stay there. If it sinks part way and one side or the top bobs up, it's nearing its expiration. If it rises to the top, it should be thrown away.

Pantry Challenge

If you've got a pantry full of food and nothing to eat, it may be time for a pantry challenge. A pantry challenge is frugal lingo for using up what you have before buying more. They've become popular with online groups like Mommysavers because they force you to work with what you have and use it creatively when you're working hard to slash your food budget.

The best time to do a pantry challenge is before you go on vacation, when you have too much on hand, or simply when your budget is especially tight. If you're short on ideas, visit supercook. com for inspiration. It searches for recipes based on the foods you have at home. The more ingredients you enter, the more options you'll have. Another option is to check out the free recipe sites mentioned on page 10. Most of them allow you to type in the ingredients you have and will give you results based on your search criteria. Or visit the Mommysavers discussion forums to ask for recipes and suggestions.

PANTRY CHALLENGE: WHAT WOULD YOU MAKE?

Available in your pantry: rice, pasta, tomato sauce, kidney beans, black beans, onions, carrots, garlic, celery, potatoes, chicken, ground beef, frozen broccoli, frozen peas, milk, butter, oil, eggs, chicken broth, cheddar cheese, Parmesan cheese, lemon juice concentrate, flour, sugar, salt and pepper.

Mommysavers.com members offered the following suggestions (visit the forums to view entire recipes):

- Beef and Cheddaroni
- Chicken Jambalaya
- Shepherd's Pie
- Quick Bolognese Sauce
- Chicken and Rice Soup
- Italian Vegetable Beef Soup
- Pasta e Fagioli Stew
- Black Bean Chicken Chili
- Cheesy Beef and Broccoli Casserole
- Cheeseburger Quiche

The Well-Equipped Kitchen

A well-equipped kitchen is imperative to the frugal cook. Besides the basics like an oven, a microwave, and silverware, there are plenty of kitchen gadgets and tools that will not only save you money but also save you time in the long run—things like a bread maker, slow cooker, and food dehydrator.

WHERE TO SHOP

THRIFT STORES AND GARAGE SALES. Many unused kitchen appliances end up at thrift stores and garage sales. You may just be lucky enough to find a bargain at up to 90 percent off the original price. If you are buying an electric appliance, be sure to ask if you can plug it in to ensure that it works prior to checking out.

$ **AMAZON.COM.** Amazon has a wide variety of cookware and appliances. Many of these items ship for free with Super Saver Shipping on a $25 purchase. Amazon also offers a range of factory-refurbished appliances for up to 60 percent off the original price.

$ **T.J. MAXX/MARSHALLS.** Look for high-quality brand-name kitchen tools and gadgets here at 20 to 60 percent off the original retail price.

$ **CRAIGSLIST, EBAY.** You can also go online to find gently used appliances and kitchen gear at great prices.

$ **KITCHEN OUTLETS.** You'll find kitchen stores at most major outlet malls.

WHEN TO BUY

Timing your purchases can save you 50 percent or more on small appliances. May and June are good times to look because these items are often promoted during Mother's Day, Father's Day, and in conjunction with wedding season. The same goes for November and December, when stores compete for your holiday gift purchases. Look for small appliances touted as door-buster promotions on Black Friday (the day after Thanksgiving).

SMALL APPLIANCES FOR THE FRUGAL KITCHEN

Consider a small appliance a good investment if it gets used, is versatile, and helps you save money. You have to take a close look at the foods you enjoy when determining if an appliance is worth the investment to you. It pays to know your family's favorite staples and eating habits. If you eat a lot of yogurt, a homemade yogurt machine may make sense for you and help save money over time. It will not convert you to a fan of yogurt if you aren't already—and it will likely be a waste of money and kitchen space.

Here are some of the more frequently mentioned appliances that can help you save:

Bread Machine

While a savvy shopper can find great deals on bread, it most likely doesn't taste nearly as good as homemade. In addition, store-bought breads contain loads of preservatives to prolong shelf life, making them easy and convenient but not nearly as tasty or healthy as home-made loaves. Plus, some of the fancier artisanal breads or healthy whole-grain loaves can cost anywhere from $2.50 to $5.00 per loaf. You can make them at home for a fraction of this price.

$ **BREAD MACHINES AREN'T JUST FOR BREAD, EITHER.** They're extremely versatile. The dough feature is a great way to simply create made-from-scratch pizza crusts, biscuits, and rolls. If you don't care for the square-shaped loaves or the hole that the machine's mixing paddle leaves behind, try using the dough feature instead. Then, bread can be popped in the oven in a bread pan or shaped like a baguette.

$ **BUY IN BULK.** If you find that you're making a lot of bread, consider buying a 50-pound bag of flour at warehouse stores like BJ's, Sam's, or Costco. Compare the unit price per pound to ensure your investment is a good one. Yeast can also be purchased in bulk, helping you save even more money. Bread flour works better for your loaves and is worth the slightly higher price. It is a high-protein flour that contains more gluten, which is vital in the rising process and creates a better texture.

$ **SLICING TIPS.** Another common complaint about bread made using a bread machine is that it is difficult to cut without its falling apart. Try adding more flour to the dough for a more dense bread, or try cutting loaves with an electric knife. Don't forget to save the crumbs (see page 209 for uses).

Bread Machine Pizza Dough

2 cups bread flour

¾ cup water

3 tablespoons olive oil

1 tablespoon bread machine yeast

1 tablespoon honey

½ teaspoon salt

Combine all ingredients and use dough setting. Dough can be frozen for later use. For best results, thaw in the refrigerator.

Slow Cooker

A slow cooker is a must-have for busy cooks interested in saving both time and money. It's great for busy nights when you don't have time for making a home-cooked dinner and can help you avoid takeout temptation. Prep work is done ahead of time, and by the time you get home, you have a hot, delicious meal waiting. A slow cooker will save you money for a number of reasons:

- A slow cooker costs less to operate than an oven, even when left on all day.
- Because of the slow cooking process, cheaper cuts of meat come out tender.
- You can save money by substituting water for broth, since the meats you're cooking will create their own juices.

TIPS FOR USE

BROWN YOUR MEAT before adding it to the slow cooker to seal in flavor and add color. Try dredging meat in flour before browning for a thicker sauce.

SAUTÉ VEGETABLES SLIGHTLY before adding to your slow cooker for a richer flavor.

SPRAY FIRST. Coat the inside of your slow cooker with nonstick cooking spray to ease cleanup. For stuck-on food, fill your slow cooker with hot water and ¼ cup baking soda and turn on high for an hour or so. Afterward you'll be able to easily wipe it clean.

DON'T OVERFILL. Avoid filling your slow cooker more than two-thirds to the top to avoid spills while cooking.

💲 **KEEP IT CLOSED.** Try not to open the lid very often. Slow cookers heat slowly and lose a lot of heat quickly, which could add an extra fifteen to twenty minutes each time you peek. That wastes not only time but electricity as well.

💲 **ADD WATER ONLY IF NECESSARY.** Typically, moisture will remain in the slow cooker as long as you don't open the lid too often. Avoid adding too much additional water to recipes.

💲 **WAIT TO ADD DAIRY PRODUCTS.** Avoid adding milk, sour cream, and yogurt to your recipe until the last fifteen minutes of cooking. Dairy products tend to separate and curdle when allowed to cook for a long time.

Slow Cooker Creamy Ranch Chicken

4 boneless skinless chicken breasts

1 dash paprika

1 1-ounce packet ranch dressing mix

2 tablespoons butter, melted

¼ teaspoon minced garlic

1 10.5-ounce can cream of chicken soup

8 ounces cream cheese, cubed

½ cup chicken broth

1/8 teaspoon dry oregano

¼ teaspoon dry parsley flakes

Wash and dry chicken breasts and place them evenly in slow cooker. Sprinkle with paprika.

Sprinkle ranch salad dressing mix over chicken. Drizzle chicken breasts with 1 tablespoon melted butter. Cover and cook on low for 4 hours. Melt remaining 1 tablespoon butter with minced garlic and sauté slightly. Add cream of chicken soup, cream cheese cubes, chicken broth, dried oregano, and dried parsley flakes. Stir on medium heat until smooth. Add mixture to slow cooker, cover again, and continue to cook on low for 1½ to two hours.

—TRUDY FLETCHER, EAST LIVERPOOL, OHIO

GET CREATIVE WITH YOUR SLOW COOKER

A slow cooker isn't just for main courses like meats, soups, and stews. You can also use it for side dishes, desserts, and other creative things. Here are just a few:

- **MAKE BAKED POTATOES** by pricking them with a fork, wrapping them in aluminum foil, and placing them in your slow cooker on low for eight to ten hours. Do not add water.
- **MAKE PERFECTLY PREPARED CORN ON THE COB** by shucking your corn, wrapping it in aluminum foil, and placing in the slow cooker, cooking on high for two hours. Do not add water.
- **MAKE SLOW COOKER APPLE CIDER** by combining 4 quarts of cider, four sticks cinnamon, and 2 teaspoons whole cloves and cooking on high for two hours.
- **USE PLAIN YOGURT AS A STARTER** to make more in your slow cooker (see page 191).

"In 2008 I had a New Year's resolution: I would use my slow cooker every single day for a year and document my results on a personal blog, crockpot365.blogspot.com. Through the course of the challenge,

I learned just how versatile and beneficial a slow cooker can be to a busy family. I discovered that not only can you cook traditional slow-cooked fare such as pot roast and stew, you can make granola, yogurt, baby food, and delicate desserts. I would not recommend attempting to hard-boil eggs, however!"

—STEPHANIE O'DEA, SAN FRANCISCO BAY AREA

Waffle Maker

Homemade waffles taste almost as great out of the freezer as they do freshly prepared. Plus, they're a lot more economical than prepackaged cereals and processed waffles, making them a frugal breakfast option. Making a big batch at once and freezing for later can be a great way to save time and money.

💲 **FREEZE THEM PROPERLY.** When freezing your waffles, allow them to cool completely and layer with wax paper to avoid having them stick together. Simply pop in the toaster when ready to reheat.

Vacuum Sealer

A vacuum sealer, sometimes called a Food Saver or a food sealer, is a great appliance to have if you buy a lot of meat in bulk that you repackage to eat later. It works with a special hose that vacuums the air out of special plastic storage bags and then seals them off.

Air is what causes food to deteriorate, so the less air surrounding your frozen food, the less likely it is to get freezer burn. Vacuum sealing what you put in the freezer helps extend its shelf life, maximizing your investment. It is especially handy if you have wild game to stockpile in your freezer.

§ **SOUS-VIDE.** Vacuum sealer owners can use this appliance to experiment with the sous-vide method of cooking, which literally means "under-vacuum" in French. Sous-vide is a method of slow-cooking vacuum-sealed foods in hot water well below the boiling point, typically around 140°F. It's an effective way of tenderizing tough cuts of meat without drying it or over-cooking it. A Google search on "sous-vide cooking" will yield additional tips and recipes.

Food Dehydrator

A food dehydrator is a great tool for preserving seasonal fruits, vegetables, and herbs to enjoy all year long.

§ **DRIED FRUITS ARE GREAT IN TRAIL MIXES** for a healthy snack.

§ **DRIED VEGETABLES CAN BE RECONSTITUTED** and used in soups and stews all year long. This is a must-have if you're a gardener.

Pressure Cooker

A pressure cooker seals off oxygen, raising the pressure and boiling point inside the vessel from the usual 212°F to about 250°F. Higher temperatures equal faster cooking. What can take an hour in a conventional oven takes about twenty minutes in a pressure cooker, making it an ideal method for cooking tougher cuts of meat in a short period of time. Because pressure cookers require less time, they also consume less energy. Foods are also cooked with less liquid and exposed to less oxygen, meaning more of the nutrients are retained in the process as well. Double bonus!

$ **BEANS UNDER PRESSURE.** Pressure cookers work especially well for cooking dried beans three times as fast as other methods. Because dried beans are so economical, this is a great tool to have in your kitchen.

Food Processor

A food processor can cut your prep time in half. Here are just a couple of ways:

$ **IT'S GREAT FOR CHOPPING ONIONS AND OTHER VEGETABLES** for soups, casseroles, and other dishes.

$ **IT MAKES GRATING CHEESE QUICK AND EASY.** You can even grate large blocks all at once and freeze for later use.

Electric Griddle

While you can easily make pancakes in a frying pan, this tool allows you to make double the amount in the same time. It also works well for bacon and hash browns. Since inexpensive models cost less than $40, a griddle is a good tool to have in your cooking arsenal. Again, consider your family's tastes and lifestyle. A griddle is likely to gather dust if you don't eat a lot of pancakes.

$ One of the best ways to save money on meals is to eat breakfast for dinner once a week.

Immersion Blender

An immersion blender has a blade at the end and can be inserted into the pot, which helps you avoid messy pouring. You can find a reliable model for under $20.

- This is great if you find you're making a lot of homemade soups and stews.
- You can also use it in a large glass for making smoothies.

Makeshift Kitchen Tools

Sometimes being a great chef simply comes down to making the most of what you already have. If you don't have all the latest cooking tools and gadgets, fear not!

Necessity really is the mother of invention.

- **BISCUIT AND COOKIE CUTTERS.** Drinking glasses can serve as biscuit and cookie cutters.

- **COOLING RACK.** A muffin pan turned upside down can double as a cooling rack.

- **ROLLING PIN.** A wine bottle can serve as a rolling pin.

- **COLANDER.** Make your own colander or strainer by punching holes in the bottom of an empty margarine tub or ice cream pail.

- **GARLIC PRESS.** no need for a garlic press—simply give the clove a good whack with the side of a knife blade. It will break open easily.

BROILING RACK. Use a metal cooling rack over a jelly roll pan. Line the pan with aluminum foil to make cleanup even easier.

FUNNEL. A cone-shaped coffee filter can make a good funnel.

VEGETABLE STEAMER. Use aluminum foil and a saucepan. Place veggies on top of aluminum foil that has been punched with small holes and fold over the sides of pan. Cover and steam.

PASTRY BAG. Make your own pastry bag for frosting (or any other garnishes) by cutting a small hole in the corner of a zippered plastic bag.

CLOTH NAPKINS. Recycle an old bedsheet into cloth napkins by cutting it into large squares and hemming the edges.

DOUBLE DUTY

These kitchen gadgets serve double duty as useful items. Here's how:

POTATO MASHER. A potato masher can create beautiful criss-cross patterns on peanut butter cookies.

VEGETABLE PEELER. A vegetable peeler can be used to create attractive garnishes such as carrot, chocolate, and cheese curls.

TOASTER. A toaster can be used to grill buns indoors. Just place the inside of the buns on top of the slots.

CHEESE GRATER. A cheese grater can be used to grate butter when casseroles instruct you to "dot" with butter.

EGG SLICER. An egg slicer can be used to cut semi-soft cheeses.

BROILER PAN. A broiler pan can be used to bake bacon in the oven.

TURKEY BASTER. Use a turkey baster to pick up an egg that has been dropped on the floor.

SCISSORS. A scissors works well for cutting pizza, chopping scallions, and snipping vents in pie crusts.

HAIR DRYER. A hair dryer can be used to lightly melt and smooth frosting on top of cakes to create a professional-looking finish.

COLANDER. A colander can serve as a bread basket—just line with an attractive cloth napkin!

CAKE STAND. A cake stand can be used as a candle holder for an attractive table centerpiece.

RICE COOKER. Your rice cooker can be used to make mashed potatoes.

COOKIE SHEET. A cookie sheet can be used as a drip tray for wet boots and shoes.

MELON BALLER. Use your melon baller to scoop out the inside of a potato when making twice-baked potatoes, to scoop out the seeds from inside a tomato, or to drop cookie dough onto baking sheets.

"An electric knife makes a great cake cutter! Rather than squashing the cake when cutting, it slices easily through, especially layered cakes, or through slices of fruit on cakes. Another cake idea is to use dental floss to cut a cake for layers. Use a piece that can wrap around the cake, with extra on the ends. Make sure it's centered around the cake to cut it evenly. Twist the ends around each other once, and pull. The floss will cut the cake cleanly and with very little in the way of crumbs."

—JENNIFER LEITCH, MORRICE, MICHIGAN

Kitchen Energy Savings

Saving money in the kitchen goes well beyond shopping and cooking. Following this advice has a big impact on the amount of electricity or water you consume, putting dollars back in your wallet.

AIR IT OUT. Arrange products within your refrigerator to allow air to circulate.

DON'T MAKE IT HARD ON YOUR FRIDGE. Avoid placing your refrigerator near a heating vent or beside the oven, which will cause it to have to work harder

ONE STOP SHOPPING. When cooking, get into the habit of getting everything you need to get out of the refrigerator in one trip to avoid opening and closing the door repeatedly.

COVER IT UP. When cooking on the range, cover pots and pans to seal in heat and reduce cooking time.

DITCH THE DISHWASHER. Run your dishwasher only when it's full, and on the lightest setting necessary.

AIR-DRY OPTIONS. Consider opening the door after the wash cycle and allowing dishes to air-dry.

CLEAN YOUR REFRIGERATOR COILS EVERY FOUR TO SIX MONTHS to keep it running efficiently.

CLEAN YOUR OVEN REGULARLY. Caked-on food on the coils will cause it to have to work harder to regulate temperatures. The best time to clean your oven is after you're done cooking with it. Because it's already hot, you'll use less energy.

AVOID OPENING THE OVEN DOOR. To check on progress, use the oven light and look through the door.

USE SMALLER APPLIANCES WHEN YOU CAN. For example, microwaves consume less energy than your oven or stovetop because they cook faster and at lower wattages.

NO RINSE. Avoid wasting water by loading dishes directly into the dishwasher without rinsing first. Many new dishwasher models have a built-in soil sensor that senses how dirty your dishes are. Think you're saving money washing dishes by hand?

Think again. Some dishwasher models use half the water you would standing over the sink.

OVENS HELP HEAT. During the winter, leave your oven door open after you're done using it to help heat your house.

CONSIDER BAKING TWO BATCHES WHEN COOKING YOUR OVEN. You'll get two meals and only be heating up your oven once.

TIPS FOR SAVING WHEN PURCHASING LARGE APPLIANCES

The average family spends $2,200 each year on energy bills, according to Energy Star, the government-sponsored program run jointly by the EPA and Department of Energy. Since you'll be spending more on energy to run your appliances over their lifetime than the initial sticker price itself, it pays to make a smart investment.

PURCHASE THE SMALLEST SIZE THAT MEETS YOUR NEEDS. Remember, it takes more energy to keep a large refrigerator cold than a smaller model.

GAS APPLIANCES COST LESS TO OPERATE THAN ELECTRIC. The additional expense of the initial purchase price of gas appliances could quickly be offset by energy savings over time.

LOOK FOR THE ENERGY STAR LABEL. Energy Star models are the most energy efficient in any product category, using 10 to 66 percent less energy than standard models.

$ **SIDE-BY-SIDE SPENDING.** A Refrigerator with a side-by-side freezer requires about 10 to 15 percent more energy to operate than one with a freezer on top. Add an ice cube maker and water dispenser and you're adding more to your electric bill as well.

$ **CHOOSE A DISHWASHER WITH A "LIGHT" OR "ENERGY SAVING" SETTING** so you're not wasting water and electricity in the drying cycle.

$ **FALL IS TYPICALLY THE BEST TIME TO PURCHASE LARGE APPLIANCES.** New models are introduced in September and October, meaning last year's models and showroom demo models end up on clearance.

Kitchen Tools: The Basics

When you're stocking your kitchen with practical tools, let these be the first on your list. These tools are a wise use of your culinary budget.

- Collander/strainer
- Mixing bowls
- Wooden spoons
- Slotted spoons
- Rubber spatula
- Whisk
- Pastry brush
- Small and medium saucepans
- Small and large frying pan
- Baking sheets
- Roasting pan
- Cutting boards
- Vegetable peeler
- Measuring cups
- Measuring spoons
- Box grater
- Serrated knife
- Large chef's knife
- Small chef's knife

Kitchen Cleanup

Although it would be nice to just shop, cook, and eat, you're not done yet. Kitchen cleanup may not be your favorite kitchen activity, but saving a few bucks here and there can certainly make it less costly.

OUT OF BOX. Shop at big-box retailers, pharmacies (see pages 72–74 on rebate programs), or even the local dollar store for cleaning products, where prices are typically cheaper than at the grocery store.

CONSIDER GENERIC AND STORE BRANDS. Compare labels. In many cases, the major difference is the scent.

READ LABELS. Look at the active ingredients in the cleaning solutions you typically use day to day. For example, if something contains ammonia as the number one ingredient, you may be able to make your own by buying plain ammonia and cutting the added expense.

OPT FOR HOMEMADE CLEANING SOLUTIONS. Not only are homemade cleaning solutions easy on the pocketbook, they're easy on the environment. Most of these homemade solutions are easy on the chemicals, making them safe for pets, children, and the environment.

LESS IS MORE. When it comes to household cleaners, don't use more than necessary. Avoid overuse by diluting certain products with water, putting soaps in a suds pump to control the amount dispensed, or making do without.

STOVE-TOP CLEANER. Baking soda is a natural abrasive that works well for cooked-on spills. Sprinkle a little baking soda on your stove top and use white vinegar to make a foaming paste. Rub and wipe off. This also works well for sink basins.

Dish Soap

> 1 bar white bar soap (Ivory works well)
> ½ gallon water

Grate soap into flakes. Pour water into large pot and place on the stove on medium to high heat. Add soap and stir to dissolve flakes. Bring to a boil for ten minutes, stirring frequently. Allow solution to cool, them pour into a container for later use.

USE A PUMP. Instead of drizzling dishwashing soap into running water, place it in a pump and just add what you need to your sponge to avoid waste.

CUTTING BOARD. Wipe with vinegar and microwave on high for one minute to kill germs and bacteria.

DRAIN CLEANER. Pour one cup baking soda down the drain, followed by one cup white vinegar. Allow the mixture to foam for a few minutes, then pour a quart of boiling water down the drain to flush it.

POTS/PANS. To remove stuck-on food from pots and pans, make a paste of water and meat tenderizer and coat stain. Allow it to sit for a few minutes then gently scrub off; the pans will look brand-new.

$ **MICROWAVE.** Mix two tablespoons vinegar with two cups of water in a microwave-safe bowl. Microwave on high for two to three minutes. Remove the bowl and wipe interior of the microwave clean.

$ **GARBAGE DISPOSAL.** Run a few pieces of lemon through your disposal every few days to keep it smelling fresh.

$ **OVEN CLEANER.** Pour salt on spills while your oven is still hot. Allow the oven to cool completely and scrape clean.

$ **FOR ELECTRIC OVENS ONLY.** Put a shallow dish of full-strength ammonia in your cold oven overnight. The fumes will loosen the grease and in the morning you'll be able to wipe clean.

$ **COFFEEMAKER.** To clean your coffeemaker, run through a solution of one part vinegar to one part water through the brew cycle every few weeks. Follow up with several cycles of plain water to flush the reservoir of any traces of vinegar.

$ **SPONGES.** Soak your sponge with white vinegar and microwave on high for one minute to kill bacteria and germs.

Multipurpose Cleaners

¼ cup baking soda
1 cup ammonia
½ cup white vinegar
1 gallon warm water

Pour solution into a plastic spray bottle to use on countertops or as an all-purpose cleaner.

> *"I use vinegar/water solution (25 percent vinegar, 75 percent water) as an all-purpose cleaner and store it in a spray bottle. A large jug of vinegar only costs about $3 and it lasts me up to five months! It only takes a couple of minutes to fill my spray bottle every other week or so, so it's time well invested."*
>
> —WENDY SPACE, MINDEN, NEBRASKA

COOKING FRUGALLY AND EFFICIENTLY

A Little Labor Can Pay Off

When purchasing food, a general rule of thumb is this: The closer it is to its natural state, the less expensive it will be. Any type of processing and packaging adds to the cost. The more you're willing to put into your food's preparation, the more money you're likely to save.

Convenience foods have become so commonplace these days that we seem to have forgotten how to make even the most basic foods, like pasta sauces, salad dressings, and breads and rolls. By learning some basic cooking techniques, you'll be equipped with the skills you need to ditch many of the convenience items you've been relying on.

While it's true that sometimes these things are more convenient and sometimes they are even cheaper when purchased in the store, sometimes you simply don't have them on hand. Having the ability to create them in a pinch will save time and money in the long run. Plus, by learning to cook more foods at home, you're avoiding preservatives and fillers and getting something much more nutritious.

MARINADES, SAUCES, AND SYRUPS

There's no need to purchase bottled marinades, sauces, and seasonings when you can make them at home quickly and easily. Many sauces on the market today contain high fructose corn syrup, and making them at home offers additional health benefits in addition to saving money.

> **ANY BASIC MARINADE CONTAINS THREE ELEMENTS:** oil (olive oil, vegetable oil, etc.), acid (lemon juice, vinegar, etc.), and seasoning (spices like mustard, garlic, pepper, etc.). By applying those principles to the ingredients you have at home, you'll be able to experiment with what you have on hand and concoct your own blends.

Ginger and Soy Marinade

- 2 teaspoons ginger
- ½ cup soy sauce
- ½ cup vegetable oil
- 2 teaspoons dry mustard
- 2 to 4 cloves garlic, coarsely chopped
- 2 tablespoons molasses
- 2 tablespoons white vinegar

This is great for grilling and can be used with a variety of different meats and vegetables.

Tex-Mex Steak Marinade

- 3 large cloves garlic, minced
- ¼ cup lime juice

2 teaspoons cumin

2 tablespoons olive oil

Wonderful for beef fajitas.

Savory Spaghetti Sauce

1 pound ground beef

1 large onion, chopped

1 clove garlic, minced

2 8-ounce cans tomato sauce

2 6-ounce cans tomato paste

1½ cups water

⅓ cup extra virgin olive oil

½ cup fresh parsley, chopped

½ teaspoon salt

¼ teaspoon pepper

Brown the hamburger and onions. Drain. Add remaining ingredients and simmer until flavors are well incorporated, approximately one hour. Serve over spaghetti noodles and top with freshly grated Parmesan cheese if desired. For a less expensive sauce, use ½ pound ground beef.

Alfredo Sauce

1 pint (16 ounces) heavy whipping cream

½ cup butter

1½ cups grated Parmesan cheese

Cracked black pepper to taste

Combine ingredients in a medium saucepan over medium heat. Cook until smooth. Serve over pasta. Add ingredients, such as chicken, shrimp, or sautéed vegetables, as desired.

Pesto

- 3 cloves garlic
- 2 cups fresh basil
- 3 tablespoons pine nuts
- ½ cup extra virgin olive oil
- ½ cup Parmesan cheese, grated
- Salt and pepper to taste

Combine in a food processor or blender. Serve over pasta, use as a salad dressing, use as a pizza topping, spread on toasted baguettes, or blend with a can of chickpeas for a pesto hummus dip. Make a big batch and freeze for later use.

Thai Peanut Sauce

- ½ cup crunchy peanut butter
- ½ cup water
- ¼ cup soy sauce
- 1 tablespoon brown sugar
- 2 tablespoons peanut or vegetable oil
- 2 or 3 cloves garlic, minced
- ½ teaspoon crushed red pepper flakes
- 2 tablespoons vinegar

Combine ingredients in a bowl. Serve with grilled chicken and pasta as a warm main course, or as a cold bowtie pasta salad tossed with red peppers, carrots, green onions, and cilantro. Simply toss the dressing with the veggies and chill.

Barbecue Sauce

1 cup ketchup

½ cup cider vinegar (white vinegar works, too)

½ cup brown sugar, packed

2 tablespoons soy sauce

2 tablespoons prepared mustard or 2 teaspoons ground mustard

1 teaspoon ground ginger

1 teaspoon garlic powder

One onion, sliced

Heat ingredients over the stove and simmer for 20 to 30 minutes. Remove onions before serving.

Cocktail Sauce

One part ketchup

One part horseradish sauce

Tabasco to taste (if desired)

Combine ingredients above.

Chocolate Sauce

½ cup unsweetened cocoa powder

1 cup water

1 cup sugar

¼ teaspoon salt

½ teaspoon vanilla

Dissolve the cocoa in water in a medium saucepan. Add sugar and salt and bring to a boil. Add vanilla and cool.

Maple Syrup

- 1½ cups white sugar
- ½ cup brown sugar
- 1 cup water
- 1 teaspoon vanilla extract
- 1 teaspoon maple flavoring

Mix sugars and water in saucepan. Heat to boiling over medium heat, stirring constantly. Remove from heat. Stir in vanilla extract and maple flavoring. Serve warm. Store in an airtight container in the refrigerator.

Thousand Island Dressing

- 1 cup mayonnaise
- ¼ cup sweet pickle relish
- ¼ cup ketchup
- One hard-cooked egg, chopped (optional)

Mix ingredients together. Season with sugar and celery seed to taste.

DAIRY PRODUCTS

Before prepackaged puddings, yogurts, and even whipped cream, families made these things from scratch. They're easy to do, and just may surprise you with their great flavor.

Buttermilk

- 1 tablespoon vinegar
- Milk to make 1 cup

Pour vinegar into measuring cup; add milk until full. You can also use lemon or cream of tartar in place of the vinegar.

Whipped Cream

½ pint heavy cream

⅓ cup sugar

Pinch salt

Pour cream into a small bowl that has been chilled for at least half an hour. Add sugar and salt. Using a whisk or blender, beat until stiff peaks form. Add more sugar to thicken if necessary.

Vanilla Pudding

2½ cups cold milk

2 tablespoons cornstarch

⅔ cup sugar

1 teaspoon vanilla

Pinch salt

Combine milk, cornstarch, and sugar in a saucepan and cook over low heat, stirring constantly, until mixture thickens. Remove from heat and stir in vanilla. For a chocolate version, add 2 tablespoons cocoa powder.

Slow Cooker Yogurt

8 cups (½ gallon) milk

½ cup plain yogurt with live cultures

Insulation for slow cooker (a thick bath towel works well)

Pour milk into slow cooker and turn on low setting. Cover and cook for 2½ to 3 hours.

Unplug slow cooker and, while still covered, allow to sit for 3 hours. Scoop out 2 cups of milk and place in a bowl. Whisk in ½ cup yogurt and return mixture to the slow cooker. Stir to combine well.

Put the lid back on the slow cooker and wrap with towel to insulate. Allow to sit overnight, or 8 hours. Place in plastic containers and refrigerate. Lasts seven to ten days.

BAKING MIXES AND SEASONINGS

A lot of these mixes and seasonings can be made in bulk and stored in airtight containers until you're ready to use them. Don't forget to label the container and include the instructions.

Crescent Rolls

2 packages active dry yeast (or bread machine yeast)

½ cup warm water

¼ cup milk

½ cup sugar

1 teaspoon salt

2 eggs

½ cup butter, softened

¼ cup shortening

4 cups all-purpose flour

This is a great basic dough recipe to use in your bread machine on the dough cycle. Bake rolls at 400°F for 12 to 15 minutes or until a light golden brown. Brush with butter while still warm.

Self-Rising Flour

1 cup all-purpose flour

1½ teaspoons baking powder

½ teaspoon salt

Mix to combine.

Baking Mix

4 cups all-purpose flour

2 tablespoons baking powder

1½ teaspoons salt

1 cup shortening

Blend all ingredients well and store in an airtight container. Use as you would regular Bisquick.

Pancake Mix

6 cups all-purpose flour

6 tablespoons baking powder

6 tablespoons sugar

2 cups powdered milk

1 tablespoon salt

Combine dry ingredients and store in an airtight container. To use, combine 1½ cups mix with 1 egg, 1 cup water, and 2 tablespoons oil. An easy way to add more whole grains to your diet is to substitute ½ cup all-purpose flour when a recipe calls for 1 cup flour.

Stuffing Mix

1 tablespoon dried celery

8 slices bread, cubed and dried (arrange on a cookie sheet over-night to dry)

2 teaspoons chicken bouillon granules

2 teaspoons onions, minced

¼ teaspoon onion powder

Cracked pepper to taste

¼ butter

⋮   1½ cups hot water

Combine dry ingredients and mix with butter and hot water.

Taco Seasoning

⋮   1 teaspoon onion powder
⋮   1 teaspoon salt
⋮   1 teaspoon cumin
⋮   1 teaspoon chili powder
⋮   1 teaspoon flour
⋮   ½ teaspoon crushed dried red pepper
⋮   ½ teaspoon garlic powder
⋮   ¼ teaspoon dried oregano

Use with one pound beef, chicken, or beans and ⅔ cup water to thicken.

Dry Onion Soup Mix

⋮   4 teaspoons instant beef bouillon
⋮   8 teaspoons dried onion, minced
⋮   1 teaspoon onion powder
⋮   ¼ teaspoon white pepper

Blend together to create the equivalent of one packet dry onion soup mix.

Ranch Mix

⋮   1 teaspoon salt
⋮   ½ teaspoon pepper
⋮   ½ teaspoon garlic powder
⋮   ½ teaspoon onion powder
⋮   2 teaspoons parsley flakes

Combine seasonings. Add 1 cup each mayonnaise (or creamy salad dressing) and buttermilk. Mix well and store in refrigerator.

Condensed Cream of Chicken Soup

1 tablespoon butter

3 tablespoons flour

½ cup chicken broth

½ cup milk

Salt and pepper to taste

Melt butter in a saucepan over medium heat. Add flour and stir until smooth. Lower heat and add the chicken broth, milk, and salt and pepper. Stir until thickened. This recipe yields the equivalent of one can of condensed soup.

Condensed Cream of Mushroom Soup

1 tablespoon butter

3 tablespoons flour

½ cup beef broth

½ cup milk

¼ teaspoon each garlic and onion powder

8 ounces fresh mushrooms, chopped and sautéed

Salt and pepper to taste

Melt butter in a saucepan over medium heat. Add flour and stir until smooth. Lower heat and add the beef broth, milk, garlic and onion powders, mushrooms, and salt and pepper. Stir until thickened. This recipe yields the equivalent of one can of condensed soup.

Mayonnaise and Aioli

1 whole egg

1 egg yolk

2 cups canola or vegetable oil

> 1 teaspoon vinegar or lemon juice
> Salt and pepper

In a food processor, blender, or mixer, combine egg and egg yolk, and slowly stream in oil. Add vinegar or lemon juice and salt and pepper to taste.

Add two peeled and crushed garlic cloves to the mixture above to create an aïoli sauce that tastes great with French fries.

> *"When my kids were young, we worked in India for nearly five years. There were certain foods that we missed so much that we learned to make them ourselves from scratch. These included bread, yogurt, maple syrup, pancake mix, tortillas, and potato chips. After we returned home at the end of our term, we bought the 'real' stuff from the grocery store and were surprised to discover we all liked our homemade items better than the store-bought stuff."*
>
> —KATHRYN HANNAH, ONTARIO, CANADA

Basic Roux

> 1 part flour
> 1 part oil or butter

Roux is a mixture of flour and fat used to thicken sauces. It's made by mixing the fat and flour in a saucepan over low heat until the desired color is reached. The less you brown the roux, the more it will thicken your sauce. The more you brown the roux, the more it will develop a nutty flavor. You can even refrigerate or freeze roux for up to two months to use later. It's great to have on hand to thicken sauces, gravies, and stews.

- Cook a white or blond roux for ten to fifteen minutes. Ideal for cheese sauces, scalloped potatoes, bisques, and lighter soups.

- Cook a medium brown roux for thirty to thirty-five minutes. Ideal for gravies and thick soups.

- Cook a dark roux for thirty-five to forty-five minutes. Great as a Cajun roux in gumbo.

BROTHS AND STOCKS

Making homemade stocks and broths is a great way to use up portions of meats and vegetables that normally get tossed away. They're easy to make and add great flavor to a variety of items, not just soups and stews.

- Cook rice in it for risottos, pilafs, and other dishes.

- Use it to thin and flavor a roux or white sauce.

Vegetable Stock

Vegetable stock is a frugal yet flavorful base for many recipes, and it can be a great way to use up vegetables. To start, begin by selecting your vegetables. Great choices include:

- Onions
- Carrots
- Celery
- Potatoes
- Leeks
- Garlic
- Peppers
- Fennel
- Tomatoes

You may want to begin by roasting the vegetables before placing them in the stockpot. Roasting them until they're caramelized creates a richer broth and fuller-bodied flavor. To do this, preheat your oven to 400°F and place carrots, onions, and garlic on a cookie sheet. Bake for thirty to forty-five minutes or until they're soft and start to brown slightly.

To create the stock, place coarsely chopped vegetables in a stockpot (or save vegetable peels and scraps to make an even thriftier version). Add seasoning to create a savory flavor.

Consider what you'll be using the stock for when you flavor it.

- If you're making minestrone, you may want to add basil and tomatoes.

- If you're making an Asian dish, consider adding ginger.

- Thyme, parsley, bay leaves, and sage are good choices in general, but mainly it's up to you.

Bring to a boil and then reduce heat. Simmer on low for one hour. Strain the vegetables from the broth using a colander, pressing down on the vegetables to get out as much flavor as possible. Discard the vegetables and allow the stock to cool.

Chicken/Turkey Stock

Put chicken or turkey bones in a large stockpot and cover with cold water. Season with salt, pepper, and vegetables like onion, garlic, carrot, and parsley if desired. Bring to a boil and then reduce heat and simmer uncovered for two hours, longer if a more concentrated stock is desired. Remove bones and strain stock. Allow to cool, then refrigerate.

- Optional: Save potato water (the water created when potatoes are boiled) to make a thicker stock.

- Slow cooker method: Use your slow cooker to simmer stocks for four to six hours on high, or eight to ten hours on low.

STORING YOUR STOCK. If you aren't going to be using the broth right away, freeze in ice cube trays or muffin tins. When frozen, pop out of the tray and store in a zippered bag for later use.

Limit Food Waste

If you think that maximizing your food budget starts and ends at the grocery store, you're wrong. In fact, a lot of the waste in your budget comes from allowing what you buy to go to waste. A University of Arizona at Tucson study found that the average family throws away 1.28 pounds of food per day, which adds up to an annual total of 470 pounds per household, or 14 percent of all food brought into the house.

To get an idea of how much your own family wastes, start tracking what you throw away over the next day or two. Make a mental note of that little bit of milk that ends up in the bottom of a drink glass, that serving of leftover casserole in the Rubbermaid container from last week, or the wilted lettuce leaves because you couldn't bear to eat another salad. It all adds up. Avoiding waste is a key strategy in saving on your grocery budget.

TIPS FOR REDUCING WASTE

FILL GLASSES HALFWAY. You can always refill.

§ **REDUCE THE SIZE OF THE RECIPES YOU PREPARE.** Make note of any recipes you frequently end up throwing away and reduce them accordingly.

§ **USE UP PERISHABLES.** Take note of which items in your refrigerator are perishable and incorporate them in your menu plans first.

IS YOUR FOOD STILL GOOD? DON'T THROW THAT OUT!

There is a public misconception that the dates on the cartons, boxes, and cans are expiration dates, but that's not always the case. "Sell-by" dates are different, and often provide some wiggle room (at least a few days) after the date for safe usage. Make sure you're aware of these dates and what they mean before you consider throwing food away.

Types of Dates

- A **"SELL-BY"** date tells the store how long to display the product for sale. You should buy the product before the date expires.
- A **"BEST IF USED BY (OR BEFORE)"** date refers to the best flavor or quality. It is not a purchase or safety date.
- A **"USE-BY" DATE** is the last date recommended for the use of the product at peak quality. The date has been determined by the manufacturer of the product.
- **CLOSED OR CODED DATES** are packing numbers for use by the manufacturer.

SOURCE: USDA FOOD SAFETY AND INSPECTION SERVICE

Leftovers

Today's leftovers can easily become tomorrow's meals. Always try to incorporate leftovers in your menu plan. However, with some creativity you don't have to feel like you're eating the same thing day in and day out. Adding new flavors is a quick and easy way to give your leftovers a makeover. Some general tips:

- **USE SEE-THROUGH CONTAINERS TO STORE LEFTOVERS** in the refrigerator so you can easily keep tabs on what's inside. That way, you're less apt to forget to eat it up.

- **PLAN ON CREATIVE WAYS TO USE UP LEFTOVERS** when you create your menu plan and grocery list.

- **GET USED TO EATING LEFTOVER MEALS FOR LUNCHES.**

- **PLAN A "LEFTOVER" NIGHT ONCE A WEEK,** preferably the night before you go grocery shopping.

- **FREEZE LEFTOVERS** to eat later on when you don't feel like cooking.

- **STORE PASTA AND SAUCE LEFTOVERS IN SEPARATE CONTAINERS** to maximize serving options.

LEFTOVER STANDARDS

No matter what leftovers you have on hand, they can usually morph into the following:

- Pizza (using leftover meats, veggies, and cheese as toppings)

- Quiche or omelets (using leftover veggies and meat)
- Potato toppers (a wide variety of sauces can be used to top a baked potato)
- Tortillas (meats and dips, along with a little lettuce, can be made into a wrap sandwich, or combine with cheese to make a burrito)
- Soups (using leftover noodles, rice, and veggies)
- Sandwich spread (a great way to use up leftover meat)

Easy Sandwich Spread

1 cup ground leftover meat

2 hard-boiled eggs, chopped

1 tablespoon mayonnaise or salad dressing

1 teaspoon pickle relish (optional)

Salt and pepper to taste

LET THE WIZARD HELP! Have three leftover ingredients and aren't sure what to make? Go online and try Big Oven's leftover wizard for some delicious options: www.bigoven.com/leftoverwizard2.aspx.

Try leftoverchef.com for inspiration. Enter the foods you want to use up in the search field and the site will suggest quick, easy, and flavorful meals based on what you have.

LEFTOVER MAKEOVERS

If you find yourself with these things in your fridge, here are some great ways to use them up:

Beef roast

- Beef barley soup
- Shred, mix with cheese and sautéed peppers, and serve on a hoagie roll
- Shred, mix with barbecue sauce, and serve on buns
- Top with mashed potatoes and gravy on bread for open-faced beef commercial sandwiches, a Midwest regional favorite.
- Chili
- Mix with beans for a burrito filling
- Beef stroganoff

Carrots

- Fried rice
- Soups and stews
- Carrot muffins and cake

Chicken

- Chicken salad
- Chicken and dumplings
- Chicken enchiladas
- Chicken tortilla soup
- Chicken fried rice
- Use as a pizza topping

Chili

- Chili dogs
- Use as a baked potato topping along with cheddar cheese
- Serve with elbow macaroni and cheese for chili mac
- Use as taco filling

Fish

- Toss with black beans and rice, lime, and cilantro for fish tacos
- Fish cakes

Ham

- Ham salad
- Potatoes au gratin with ham
- Cuban sandwiches or grilled ham and Swiss
- Eggs Benedict
- Fettuccine Alfredo with Peas and Ham
- Omelets or egg bake
- Breakfast burritos or breakfast pizza
- Use in soups: black bean, lentil, potato
- Toss with pasta or mac and cheese
- JFK (Just for Kids): green eggs and ham

Lettuce and salad greens

- Use in soups with noodles and chicken broth

Macaroni and cheese

- Fried mac and cheese
- Goulash (add tomatoes, onions, and ground beef)

Mashed potatoes

- Gnocchi (potato dumplings)
- Potato cakes
- Shepherd's pie
- Use to thicken soups and stews

Meatloaf

- Meatloaf sandwiches
- Crumble in spaghetti sauce to make spaghetti with "meatballs"
- Use as the meat in tacos or enchiladas

Pork

- Dice to use in fried rice
- Add to Ramen noodles and top with green onions
- Shred and add barbecue sauce for sandwiches
- Pork and beans

Rice

- Fried rice
- Rice pudding
- Make into a crust for a quiche

Rice Balls

1 cup leftover rice

2 eggs

1/3 cup Parmesan cheese, grated

4 ounces Mozzarella cheese, cut into half-inch cubes

11/2 cup dried Italian breadcrumbs

1/2 cup extra virgin olive oil

Combine rice, eggs, and Parmesan cheese in a bowl. Form the rice mixture into golf ball–shaped balls. Tuck the Mozzarella inside.

Roll the balls in breadcrumbs and sauté in olive oil until the outside is crisp and the cheese has melted.

Spaghetti sauce

- Use as a sauce for a homemade pizza
- Pour over roast in a slow cooker to add Italian flavor
- Top ground beef with spaghetti sauce and melt mozzarella cheese to create an Italian burger
- Bake chicken breasts until done and then top with leftover spaghetti sauce and mozzarella cheese

Taco filling

- Use in Mexican rice
- Use as a pizza topping
- Mix with refried beans and make enchiladas
- Taco salads
- Use as a potato topper with cheddar cheese and sour cream
- Mix with tater tots and top with cheddar cheese

Turkey

- Turkey salad
- Create a hot turkey sandwich topped with mashed potatoes and gravy
- Turkey à la king

Turkey Salad

3 cups turkey, diced

2 large stalks celery, diced

1 red bell pepper, seeded and diced

½ onion, diced

6 tablespoons mayonnaise

6 tablespoons sour cream

½ cup feta cheese, crumbled

2 teaspoons dill weed

Mix all ingredients and chill thoroughly before serving. Serve on a bed of lettuce.

- You can use turkey for basically anything you would use chicken for. See "Chicken" above.

Vegetables

- Soups and stews—keep in a storage container in your fridge to make veggie soup later on

§ Shepherd's pie

§ Veggie pizza

§ Veggie omelets

> *"I like to make a quick soup lunch for my son and myself at least twice a week. I start with generic condensed soup ($0.59) and add any leftover meat, rice, pasta, and vegetables I have in the refrigerator. If I don't have leftover veggies, I use a can of generic mixed vegetables ($0.69) from the store. Quick, tasty, and frugal!"*
>
> —JAMIE SNIDER, STERLING, ALASKA

STORING LEFTOVERS

§ **USE AIRTIGHT CONTAINERS.** Store leftovers in airtight, leak-proof containers or bags within two hours of cooking. Leave space around them in the refrigerator to allow cool air to circulate.

§ **USE SMALL CONTAINERS.** Choose small containers just large enough to accommodate what you're storing. If they're too large, the excess air will cause food to deteriorate more rapidly.

§ **STORE ITEMS INDIVIDUALLY.** Avoid storing multiple items in the same container so as to not affect taste.

§ **REMOVE ITEMS FROM TIN CANS.** Otherwise, you may find that they take on a metallic taste.

§ **CONSIDER REUSING GLASS JARS.** If you're concerned about the effect of plastics on your health, put your leftovers in recycled glass jars. Use jars from pasta sauce, salsa, and pickles. Wide-mouthed jars work especially well. Soak the jars in hot water for an hour or so to remove the labels. Just be sure to remove the lid before placing in the microwave. Additionally, they're free!

Recommended Refrigerator Storage Times

- Soups and stews: three to four days
- Gravy and meat broth: one to two days
- Cooked turkey, meat, and meat dishes: three to four days
- Cooked poultry dishes: three to four days
- Casseroles: three to four days
- Luncheon meats: opened package, three to five days; unopened package, two weeks
- Pasta and potato salads: three to five days

SOURCE: UNIVERSITY OF MINNESOTA EXTENSION

Don't Throw Those Things Away!

Not only can you create brand-new meals out of leftovers, but you can also create other useful items from certain things you typically discard. Here are some suggestions on how to look at your kitchen waste in a new way.

Bacon bits/grease

- Bacon bits can be stored in a freezer bag for up to three months (be sure to label the bag with the start date) and add to it whenever you have leftover pieces of bacon.
- Save bacon grease in a jar in your refrigerator. In small amounts, bacon fat adds great flavor when used to cook potatoes, eggs, soups, stews, salads, and pasta.

Overripe bananas

- Banana breads, muffins, bars, and pancakes
- Fruit smoothies

Bread, rolls, buns, and breadcrumbs

- Bread pudding
- Egg bake or quiche
- Croutons
- Stuffing
- French toast
- Garlic bread
- Filler for quiches, meatloaf
- Topping for casseroles
- Breading for chicken, fish, or other meats
- Use cookie, candy bar, and brownie crumbs as an ice cream topping

Breadcrumb Cookies

1¼ cups sugar

½ cup milk

1 egg

⅔ cup melted margarine or shortening

1½ teaspoon vanilla

1¼ cups flour

½ teaspoon salt

½ teaspoon baking powder

⅓ cup cocoa

2 cups breadcrumbs

Cream sugar, milk, egg, vanilla, and butter together. Add dry ingredients and drop by spoonfuls onto ungreased cookie sheet. Bake 15 minutes or until done.

SOURCE: RECIPE ADAPTED FROM *THE COMPLETE TIGHTWAD GAZETTE*

BY AMY DACYCZYN

Broccoli stems

- Peel tough stems with a vegetable peeler and chop. The inside of the stem is very tender when cooked and makes a great addition to casseroles, soups, or omelets.

Brown sugar

- Soften rock-hard brown sugar by adding a few drops of water and microwaving on medium for about fifteen or twenty seconds. Or put a slice of bread in a ziptop bag with the sugar. The sugar will absorb the bread's moisture. You can also try placing an apple slice in the bag of brown sugar to soften it.

Cheese rinds

- Add rind to simmering potatoes, pasta, beans, rice, or soup to add a rich flavor

Chicken carcass

- Throw bones and carcass into a pot with sliced onion, chopped celery, and a bay leaf to make chicken stock (see page 198).

Coffee

- Make iced coffee cubes to throw in too-hot coffee cups
- Use as a marinade for steak; makes an earthy-tasting gravy
- Use a little bit in chocolate cake and brownie recipes to add a richer mocha flavor
- Tiramisu

Cornflake crumbs

- Crush on top of a casserole and drizzle with butter.

Cranberry sauce

- Mix with cream cheese and spread over a toasted bagel.

Frosting

- Frost graham crackers, vanilla wafers, or cookies and make into a "sandwich." Or dip pretzels in it. Stick in the freezer to enjoy later.

Fruit syrup

- We're talking about the syrup that is in canned peaches, pears, and other fruit. Freeze it in ice cube trays, remove, and store in freezer bags. This can be used in:
  - Gelatin salads
  - Fruit smoothies
  - Plain yogurt to add flavor
  - Cornstarch to make a glaze
  - Salad dressings

Gravy

- Freeze gravy in ice cube trays for later use. Its uses include:
  - A base for broths in soups and stews
  - A replacement for cream soups in casseroles
  - In homemade pot pies
  - A topping for French fries or rice (and of course, mashed potatoes)

Individual egg whites and yolks

- Use egg whites to make meringue cookies. The egg whites can be dropped into an ice cube tray (one per slot) and frozen for later use.
- Use yolks to make vanilla pudding.
- Whites and yolks can be used in fried rice.
- Use an egg white that's been beaten until frothy as a facial to tighten skin.

Melted ice cream

⚜ Refreeze melted ice cream in a premade pie crust for a delicious dessert.

⚜ Blend with ripe fruit to create a sweet yet healthy smoothie drink.

Mushroom stems

⚜ Make duxelles by mincing mushroom stems and sautéeing with shallots in butter until soft and dry. Use to flavor sauces, stuffing, or soups.

Onions

⚜ If you've chopped too many onions, store the excess in a plastic bag in the freezer. They'll remain fresh for one month. To thaw, immerse the bag in cool water.

Orange peels

⚜ An orange or grapefruit cut in half and hollowed out can make an attractive serving bowl for sherbet or ice cream.

⚜ Place in a pot of water and simmer for an air freshener.

⚜ Use dried orange peel as a firestarter or kindling due to its high oil content.

⚜ Scrape the rind with a zester, dry overnight, and store in an airtight container. Use leftover zest to add flavor to sauces, soups, and salads.

Pickle juice

⚜ Pickle juice can be used to marinade pork chops, steaks, and other cuts of meat. The acidity tenderizes the meat.

Potato chip crumbs

⚜ Use as a casserole topper.

Potato water

⚜ Use to thicken soups, stews, and gravies.

⚜ Use in breads and rolls.

Raisins

⚜ Soften rock-hard raisins by microwaving in a bowl of water in thirty-second intervals until tender.

Shrimp

⚜ Boil shrimp shells to make shrimp broth to use in gumbo.

Stale sodas or beer

⚜ Stale cola can be used in the slow cooker with ketchup as a marinade to help tenderize cheap cuts of meat.

⚜ Use to make a batter for fish

⚜ Use to make bread.

Beer Bread

3 cups self-rising flour

⅓ cup sugar

1 12-ounce can beer or carbonated soft drink

Bake at 375°F for 45 minutes or until brown. Brush with butter. The kind of beer/soda you use creates either a light or dark flavor. A light beer will produce a light bread, a dark beer a darker, more flavorful bread. Don't worry, the alcohol burns off when you bake it.

Sauces, pastes, and purees

⚜ Freeze in an ice cube tray and then pop out when frozen. Stick in a small freezer bag and label with the contents to use at a later date.

Yogurt

⚜ Use as a starter for a new batch of yogurt (see page 191).

Wine

⚜ Freeze in ice cube trays, remove, and store in freezer bags. You'll have wine ready for use in recipes. Wine adds great flavor to casseroles, soups, stews, broths, and gravies. You can also pair two parts wine with one part club soda for a refreshing spritzer. Note that due to the alcohol content in the wine, it has a lower freezing point than other liquids. It is best frozen at temperatures in the high teens to low 20s.

If you enjoy wine but frequently find yourself with some remaining in the bottle, consider buying a Wine Saver, a product manufactured by Vacu Vin that's priced under $15. It works by vacuuming the remaining air out of the bottle of wine and sealing it off, which helps it last longer in your refrigerator while preserving the taste.

TURN YOUR TRASH INTO CASH! Terracycle, a self-proclaimed eco-capitalist company, will donate cold, hard cash to the school or nonprofit organization of your choice when you mail in your used juice pouches, cookie wrappers, chip bags, and other consumer waste. In turn, these waste products are used to create unique products such as backpacks, lunchboxes, and totes. To find out more, visit www.terracycle.net.

CREATE YOUR OWN COMPOST BIN

If you have a garden—anything from a container garden to a more complex garden—be sure to save leftover kitchen scraps for compost. Compost, which is simply decayed plant matter, enriches soil with nutrients and fertilizes growing plants. Not only that, it helps reduce the amount of waste that ends up in landfills, making it a very eco-friendly thing to create.

Make your compost easy on yourself. Start by throwing items in a coffee can under the sink, and then out to a larger bin in your yard. You can use a plastic garbage can with holes drilled on the sides for aeration or make your own compost bin out of wood. Instructions are readily available on the Internet.

What to include:
- Leftover fruit and veggie scraps
- Coffee grounds
- Grass clippings

What not to include:
- Animal products
- Fish
- Dairy products
- Meat

Make sure to keep compost moist, but not soggy. If the compost pile begins to smell bad, it could be a sign that it is too wet. Don't add anything to the pile for a few days and allow the compost to dry out a bit. Make sure you "stir" the compost every few days to allow for faster decomposition.

Compost should be ready in about six to eight weeks.

NEW USES FOR FOOD CONTAINERS

Don't throw away those empty food containers! You can use them to store leftovers, store household items, and even turn them into simple toys for your children. Here are some suggestions:

Berry Baskets
- Thread with ribbon or raffia to create a small gift basket.
- Use them as pantry storage to hold seasoning packets.
- Use as a suet holder for birds by joining two baskets together with pipe cleaners or twist-ties.

Bread Bags

- Use as sandwich bags.
- Use to dispose of dirty diapers.
- Throw in your beach bag to hold wet swimsuits.
- Use as a trash bag in the car.
- Create a homemade jump rope by tying bread bags end to end.

Bread Clips

- Use as a bookmark.
- Use to label electrical cords and cables so they're easily identifiable.
- Use to scrape burned-on food off pans.

Bottles

- Cut the bottom off a plastic bottle to use the top as a funnel.

Butter or Margarine Wrappers

- Use to grease pans.
- Use to press down Rice Krispy Treats in the pan.

Cereal Bags

- Use as a freezer bag to store meats.
- Use to coat meats and fish with breading (think Shake and Bake).
- Use to crush nuts or make cracker crumbs with a rolling pin.

Cereal Boxes

- Cover with contact paper and use to store back issues of your favorite magazines.

Use as toy blocks.

Use to keep envelopes stiff when mailing photographs.

Egg Cartons

Use to store golf balls.

Use to start plant seeds in the winter before planting in the spring.

Use to organize earrings, necklaces, and jewelry in your drawer.

Ice Cream Buckets

Store crayons and markers.

Create a toy drum for a baby by covering the bucket with contact paper and using a wooden spoon as a drumstick.

Margarine Tubs

Use to store leftover foods in the refrigerator.

Use to transport water for pets when you're on a car trip.

Poke holes in the bottom and use for small houseplants.

Let the kids use as bath or sandbox toys.

Mesh Produce Bags (the kind that oranges, onions, and potatoes come in)

Use a rubber band to tie off and use as a scouring pad.

Use to hang tub toys to dry.

Use to store cookie cutters.

Metal Juice Lids

Stick a magnet on the back and a photo or stickers on the front for attractive refrigerator magnets.

◊ Create your own memory game with kids. Create pairs of two matching sets with stickers, turn upside down, and have kids match the sets by memory.

Milk Jugs

◊ Cut the bottom third off and use as a bowl for a dog or cat.

◊ Cut off the bottom 1½ inches of the milk jug (there is typically a line at this point on most jugs). Pairing the remainder with a tennis ball, you now have a ball catcher game to use in the backyard or at the beach.

◊ Follow the directions above to create an all-purpose scoop that can be used in the sandbox, at the beach, or in the snow.

Oatmeal Containers

◊ Use as a mini trash can for paper on a desk or in the car.

◊ Use to make a homemade doll cradle.

Paper Towel Tubes

◊ Use to keep extension cords neat and organized in drawers.

◊ Use to store cutlery in a drawer to avoid cuts.

◊ Stuff with shredded newspaper to make a firestarter for your campfire or fireplace.

◊ Use to store plastic bags. Keep one tucked under the front seat of your car to dispose of garbage or in the bathrooms to use as trash can liners.

Plastic Cups

❧ Can be run through the dishwasher on the top rack and used again.

Plastic Lids

❧ Use under plants to protect wood and catch drips.

❧ Use in the bathroom as soap holders or under metal cans to avoid rust marks.

Pringles Cans

❧ Use for storing string or yarn—poke a hole in the lid and string the yarn through it.

❧ Use for storing or transporting homemade cookies.

Potato Chip Bags

❧ Turn the chip bags with silver foil lining inside out, wipe clean, and use to wrap a small gift.

Squeeze Bottles

❧ Can be used as bathtub and pool toys.

❧ Fill with water and a few drops of food coloring and use to "paint" the snow in the winter.

❧ Use to squirt frosting onto a cake.

Yogurt and Pudding Containers

❧ Use to start seeds in the winter before planting in the spring.

Wine Corks

- Hot-glue them inside a frame (minus the glass) to create a bulletin board or trivet.
- Use them to label appetizers and foods at a party or potluck. Cut a slit in the narrow end, and insert an index card with the name of the dish you're serving.

The only reason to throw away plastic zipper bags is if they are damaged or if meat has been stored in them. Otherwise, they're perfectly reusable. Wash them out in the sink, and try this easy tip for drying them: Create a drying rack by inserting some chopsticks or wooden spoons in a glass jar, and hang the bags on them to air-dry.

Freezing, Canning, and Preserving Foods
USING YOUR FREEZER TO SAVE MONEY

Your freezer makes it possible for you to buy in bulk, save leftovers, and store perishable items you find on sale so that you can stock up when you find a bargain. Your freezer also allows you to cook meals ahead of time and have them at the ready on nights you simply don't feel like cooking. If you have room for it, a chest freezer can be one of the best investments to make when saving money on food. But a regular-size freezer works great too.

Here are some tips to make the most of yours:

- **A FULL FREEZER WILL CONSUME LESS ENERGY THAN AN EMPTY ONE.** Fill your freezer with ice or frozen jugs of water to help reduce your electric bill. This also serves the purpose of raising the "floor" of your freezer to make it easier to reach things at the bottom. Don't overload it, however. It will be harder to regulate temperature.

KEEP A THERMOMETER IN THE FREEZER. This will help you keep tabs on the temperature. If it's set too cold, you're wasting electricity.

STORE THINGS FLAT SO THAT THEY CAN BE EASILY STACKED. Freezer bags are great for this purpose. Make sure you squeeze the excess air out of them and then lay them flat to freeze. When they're frozen they'll look like a book. Keep a permanent marker in the box along with your freezer bags to label the contents as well as the date frozen.

MILK CRATES CAN HELP YOU ORGANIZE YOUR FREEZER. Store like items together, such as frozen veggies in one, frozen meats in another. Then, simply lift the crate out to get what you need.

WITH COOKED MEAT, REMOVE ALL FAT BEFORE FREEZING. Fat deteriorates more quickly.

TREAT YOUR FREEZER AS AN EXTENSION OF YOUR PANTRY. Keep some frozen entrées tucked away for nights you simply don't feel like cooking. They're almost always cheaper than eating out and sometimes can cost about the same as cooking at home.

$ **ORGANIZE.** One big caveat of chest-type freezers is that it's hard to reach the bottom and manage inventory. Making sure your freezer is organized can help you avoid freezer burn and save even more time and money.

$ **KEEP AN INVENTORY OF YOUR FREEZER CONTENTS.** Check things off as you use them as well as when they're added. Create one in a simple spreadsheet form or find one online by searching "printable freezer inventory."

$ **MAKE SURE YOU USE THINGS UP PROMPTLY.** While they're not necessarily unsafe if left a long time, the quality of taste can drop off considerably.

Freezer-Friendly Ideas

A wide variety of foods can be stored in the freezer. Just make sure you know how long they'll last, and make sure you use them up accordingly (see the chart on page 225).

$ **MEATS ARE ONE OF THE MOST EXPENSIVE ITEMS** on your grocery budget. Buy when prices hit rock bottom and freeze what you can't eat right away.

$ **BANANAS CAN BE FROZEN IN THEIR PEELS** to be used later in banana bread and fruit smoothies.

$ **FREEZE THE BONES.** When you cook a whole chicken, turkey, ham, or other piece of meat, store the bones in the freezer until you have time to create homemade stock. When it's done, store the stock in the freezer as well.

FREEZE COOKIE DOUGH. If you don't want to bake dozens of cookies at once, store the dough in the freezer and only bake what you'll need.

TEN WAYS TO USE FROZEN BROWNED GROUND BEEF

Buy five-pound packs of ground beef when it's on sale and brown with chopped onion in a large frying pan. Drain fat and freeze in half-pound or one-pound portions and you've got a head start on the following family favorites:

- Tacos
- Spaghetti with meat sauce
- Shepherd's pie
- Goulash
- Lasagna
- Chili
- Tater tot casserole
- Sloppy Joes
- Pizza
- Beef stroganoff

TEN WAYS TO USE FROZEN COOKED CHICKEN

Get a jump on meal preparation by dicing a large pack of chicken breasts you've found on sale, browning them, and storing in your freezer in half-pound or one-pound packs. Pull them out and you're ready to make:

- Enchiladas or burritos
- Chicken noodle soup
- Chicken tetrazzini
- Chicken and rice
- Pasta with chicken and alfredo sauce
- Stir-fry
- Chicken pasta salad
- Chicken tortilla soup
- Chicken pot pie
- Chicken curry

Do Not Freeze

- Cottage cheese
- Fruits: apricots, citrus fruits, kiwis, pears
- Eggs, in the shell or hard-boiled
- Completely cooked pasta (becomes mushy when thawed)
- Vegetables with high water content such as avocados, lettuce, celery, and cucumbers (they tend to get limp)
- Potatoes (they become mushy)
- Fried foods
- Sour cream (it tends to separate)

- Yogurt
- Mayonnaise (although it's fine to freeze a sandwich that has mayonnaise on it)
- Pudding or custard (egg-based products have a tendency to curdle when thawed)

HOW LONG WILL FROZEN FOOD KEEP?

Item	Months	Item	Months
Bacon and sausage	1 to 2	Meat, uncooked ground	3 to 4
Casseroles	2 to 3	Meat, cooked	2 to 3
Egg whites or egg substitutes	12	Poultry, uncooked whole	12
Frozen dinners and entrées	3 to 4	Poultry, uncooked parts	9
Gravies	2 to 3	Poultry, uncooked giblets	3 to 4
Ham, hot dogs, and lunchmeats	1 to 2	Poultry, cooked	4
Meat, uncooked roasts	4 to 12	Soups and stews	2 to 3
Meat, uncooked steaks or chops	4 to 12	Wild game, uncooked	8 to 12

SOURCE: U.S. DEPARTMENT OF AGRICULTURE'S FOOD SAFETY

AND INSPECTION SERVICE

WORD TO THE WISE. Never use glass jars in the freezer unless the label specifically states that the container is freezer-safe. Expansion of the contents could cause the glass to shatter.

HOME CANNING

The process of home canning involves placing food in sterilized containers and heating them to a temperature that kills bacteria. Next, oxygen is removed and a tight seal is formed as the jars cool. It's a great way to preserve seasonal produce to enjoy throughout the year when prices are higher. Strawberries, for example, are quite expensive during the winter but affordable in the spring and summer. That's the time to stock up and turn them into jams and jellies that will last all winter long.

$ **WATER-BATH CANNING.** Foods high in acid, such as tomatoes, jams, jellies, and pickles, do not need to undergo the pressure canning process. Instead, they are placed in a large pot of hot water, brought to the boiling point (212°F), and cooked for a specified amount of time.

$ **PRESSURE CANNING.** Foods low in acid, such as vegetables, meat, poultry, and seafood, need to be canned with a special pressure canner in order to ensure that bacteria and toxins that cause botulism have been completely removed. Jars are placed in 2 to 3 inches of water within the pressure canner and heated to at least 240°F.

Canning Dos and Don'ts

$ **TAKE A CLASS.** Do look into canning classes through community education and extension services.

$ **DO LOOK FOR GENTLY USED SUPPLIES.** Thrift stores, rummage sales, and sites like eBay and Craigslist can be inexpensive sources for canning supplies.

$ **DON'T TRY TO ALTER RECIPES.** Canning recipes have been formulated with exacting ratios to ensure safety and quality, and modifying them can put your health at risk.

$ **DO BUY NEW LIDS EACH YEAR.** Buy them early in the canning season (they may not be available later on).

$ **STICK TO RELIABLE RESOURCES AND RECIPES** such as those found in the Ball Blue Book, county and university educational booklets, and websites with the .edu extension.

$ **VISIT THESE WEBSITES FOR MORE INFORMATION:**
  $ National Center for Home Food Preservation: www.uga.edu/nchfp/how/general.html
  $ Pick Your Own: www.pickyourown.org/canningresources.htm

Fast and Frugal: Saving Time (and Money) in the Kitchen

Creating delicious, healthy foods doesn't have to mean spending a lot of time in the kitchen. With a little organization and planning, you can greatly simplify your cooking routine and come up with great-tasting meals.

§ **START A COOKING GROUP.** Offer to cook a meal for another family in your neighborhood once a week (or once a month; whatever you determine in advance) and have them do the same for you. Cooking a double batch doesn't mean twice the work. Leverage your time in the kitchen and make someone else's life a little bit easier at the same time.

"Since my playgroup already did a cookie swap around the holidays, we decided to give a 'dinner swap' a try as well. I enjoy it because I only have to cook once and get four meals to stash away for later, which is a huge time-saver. I also get to try new meals or enjoy recipes that never quite turned out right for me.

The event is organized on meetup.com, where we put the dinner swap event on the calendar and write details about our family's dietary preferences and allergies on the message board. Next, each mom indicates what dish she'll be preparing. If five moms are swapping, each participant needs to make at least four other meals to exchange, freeze them, then bring them to the swap night. To make it even easier, we also state that whatever bakeware/plates you use do not have to be returned. We all go home with a nice variety of meals ready to eat!"

—AMANDA OLMSTEAD MACIK, NILES, OHIO

§ **CONVENIENCE FOODS.** Stock up on frozen meals when you see them on sale at your supermarket. Look for coupons in your Sunday paper and online for other convenient dinners and box meals so you'll be stocked when you simply don't feel like cooking. While they're not always the best bargain, they're usually cheaper than hitting the drive-thru.

INVEST IN TIME-SAVING APPLIANCES. Use appliances like bread machines with a timer and slow cookers to save time in the kitchen. Set them to cook while you're at work, and you'll return home to a great-tasting meal. Pressure cookers also allow you to cook meals in less time than the traditional oven method. (See page 147 for more tips on the well-stocked kitchen.)

CREATE A LIST OF TEN. Create a list of ten meals your family enjoys that take ten minutes or less to prepare. Include meals with ingredients that are easy to store so that you are sure to have ingredients on hand. Here's an example:

1. Fish—Fish filets can be sautéed, broiled, or grilled within a matter of minutes. Serve with steamed veggies and you have a quick and healthy meal.
2. Grilled cheese—Served with tomato soup, grilled cheese sandwiches are the ultimate quick comfort-food meal.
3. Tuna sandwiches—Mix a can of good tuna with mayo and a little chopped onion and celery to make tuna sandwiches.
4. Crab legs—Buy these when they're on sale and you'll have a quick and special meal for date nights at home.
5. Quesadillas—A vegetarian version with cheddar cheese and black beans can be made in just minutes. Serve with salsa and sour cream.

6. Waffles or pancakes—They're not just for breakfast! Adding these to your dinner menus can help save both time and money.

7. Pasta primavera—Toss pasta with veggies like mushrooms, onions, and tomatoes. A simple sauce can be created by melting butter and adding a little Parmesan cheese.

8. Easy jambalaya—Quick-cooking rice, black beans, shrimp, and sausage along with Tabasco to taste make a quick and easy jambalaya.

9. Egg sandwiches—Fried eggs on an English muffin topped with a slice of American cheese makes a filling dinner.

10. Meatballs—Meatballs are a versatile food to keep in your freezer, whether you buy bagged meatballs or prepare them yourself. Use them with spaghetti sauce and noodles, meatball subs, or with cream of mushroom soup over mashed potatoes for meatballs and gravy.

TAKE ADVANTAGE OF YOUR SUPERMARKET SALAD BAR. Your supermarket salad bar isn't just for salads. It's filled with items like presliced mushrooms, green peppers, and onions that can be tossed in a stir-fry; marinated olives and crudités for entertaining guests; and fruit toppings that can be drizzled over desserts. While it's generally still a high-profit center for the store, you get to realize the time savings. Plus, it's great if you only need a small amount of a certain item.

PREP IN ADVANCE. After you've created your weekly menu plan, do as much of the slicing, dicing, and shredding as possible ahead of time. Not only will you save time on prep work, but you'll also only be getting utensils like cutting boards, food processors, and graters messy once, which translates to less cleanup time.

- When buying family-size portions of ground beef, brown five pounds at once and store in quart-size freezer bags to use later. Dice and store leftover chicken and turkey as well (see meal ideas starting on page 202).

- Chop all the onions you'll need for the week at the same time and store in the refrigerator. The same goes for celery, carrots, and green peppers. Consider investing in a food chopper (under $20) to save even more time.

- If your family takes bagged lunches to school or work, make as many meals as possible ahead of time as well so family members can just grab and go.

 **BUT I DON'T COOK!**

Even if you don't cook, you can still create healthy meals at home quickly and inexpensively. Knowing which products to buy and how to use them can help you save as much as possible.

Shop for Nearly Homemade Products

A multitude of products exist within the grocery aisles to help the reluctant chef prepare meals easily and quickly at home. Buying these products instead of indulging in a take-out or restaurant habit can help save money on your overall food bill. Even the most seasoned chefs may benefit from having some of them on hand for nights when cooking just isn't at the top of the priority list. Among them:

- Steam-and-mash potatoes
- Frozen entrées
- Boxed dinners
- Jarred sauces
- Frozen slow cooker meals
- Refrigerated bread dough, rolls, and biscuits

- Texas toast and/or bruschetta
- Frozen ravioli and tortellini
- Veggie "steamers"

THE RELUCTANT CHEF IS A GREAT CANDIDATE FOR COUPON CLIP-PING. More and more "nearly" homemade products are being introduced to the marketplace every month, and frequently manufacturers issue coupons to encourage people to try them. Look for coupons in the Sunday paper and online.

Assembly Line

Consider assembling foods at home rather than eating out. Take apple pie, for example. You can assemble one yourself at home with a premade pie crust and a can of pie filling. The cost will be less than if you were to purchase its frozen counterpart. The same goes for homemade pizza. Buy a pizza crust, a jar of sauce, and some high-quality toppings and you have an easy and healthy meal.

Easy assemble-at-home foods:
- Sandwiches
- Pasta with jarred sauce
- Pita sandwiches
- Tortilla wraps
- Canned soups, stews, and chili
- Meats on the grill (investing in a small countertop grill can be a good idea for reluctant cooks)

Ease into Cooking

Learning to add a couple of ingredients to convenience foods and freezer staples is another great way to ease into cooking. Sometimes just adding an ingredient or two can turn something ordinary into an impressive dish, regardless of your culinary skills.

PIZZA

An ordinary plain cheese pizza can be transformed into gourmet fare by adding a few premium toppings such as:

- Black olives, sun-dried tomatoes, and feta cheese
- Sliced tomatoes, fresh basil, and mozzarella cheese
- Mushrooms, onions, broccoli, and spinach

> *"Our family has pizza every Friday night. Prior to discovering Aldi, pizza cost $7.99 each, and we would have to buy two in order to feed the four of us. At Aldi I can buy a huge fresh pizza for just $6.89 that feeds our entire family. With the money we are saving on just pizza, we can add our own gourmet toppings and still have money left over. It tastes like it came from the pizza shop in town!"*
>
> —MARIE LAUCIUS, LINDEN, NEW JERSEY

SPAGHETTI SAUCE

Regular jars of inexpensive spaghetti sauce can be used to create something special:

- Add black olives and capers to create pasta puttanesca.
- Pour over chicken breasts and bake for chicken marinara.

- Mix one part spaghetti sauce with one part ricotta cheese for a yummy sauce to serve over ziti noodles.
- Pour over a roast and cook in the slow cooker all day.

FROZEN MEATBALLS

Besides paired with spaghetti and marinara sauce, frozen meatballs can be used for these easy meals:

- Make a simple version of Swedish meatballs by combining frozen meatballs with two 10.5-ounce cans cream of mushroom soup (or see page 195 to make your own), an 8-ounce carton of sour cream, and 2 teaspoons soy sauce. Serve over egg noodles.

- Cut in half and use as a pizza topping.

- Top with one cup spaghetti sauce, Provolone or Monterrey Jack cheese, and serve on toasted hoagie rolls.

CHICKEN BREASTS

Frozen chicken breasts can be thawed and used to make these easy dishes:

- Sprinkle with taco seasoning (see page 194 to make your own) and one cup of salsa, then bake at 350°F for twenty-five minutes. Top with cheddar and serve with sour cream.

- Place four chicken breasts in the slow cooker with one 10.5-ounce can condensed cream of Cheddar soup, ½ cup milk, garlic powder, and cracked pepper to taste. Cook on low all day, until chicken shreds easily and can be served on buns or in tortillas.

- Place four chicken breasts over a box of prepared stuffing mix (see page 193 to make your own) in a greased glass baking dish. Cover with one 10.5-ounce can cream of chicken or mushroom soup, and top with Swiss cheese. Bake at 325°F for one hour.

FROZEN PRECOOKED SHRIMP

Shrimp can be a frugal mainstay if purchased during BOGO (buy one, get one free) sales and used along with other frugal ingredients.

- An easy shrimp scampi is made by melting ⅓ cup butter in a frying pan and sautéeing four to six cloves minced garlic for two minutes. Toss in shrimp, 1 tablespoon lemon juice concentrate, ¼ cup white wine, and ¼ cup fresh chopped parsley. Serve with pasta.

- Stir-fry with a bag of mixed veggies and serve over rice. Season with teriyaki sauce.

- Go Creole by pairing shrimp with the "trinity" (equal parts diced green pepper, celery, and onion). Sauté the veggies in olive oil until translucent, and then add shrimp. Add ¼ cup tomato sauce and season with cracked pepper, garlic powder, and cayenne for a little zip. Serve over rice.

JARRED ALFREDO SAUCE

Alfredo sauce is great to stockpile when prices are low, and can be used in a wide variety of meals besides traditional pasta dishes.

- Use as a sauce for a "white" pizza that you top with ingredients such as chicken, shrimp, onion, mushrooms, and red peppers.

- For a cheesy potato casserole, combine one jar Alfredo sauce with one cup milk. Layer the following ingredients in a baking dish: 3 pounds potatoes, peeled and thinly sliced; one bag frozen broccoli; and 1 cup diced chicken or turkey. Season with salt and pepper and garlic powder if desired. Pour sauce over the top and cover with mozzarella cheese. Bake at 350°F for one hour.

- Make these recipes even more frugal by making your own seasoning mixes, stuffing, and condensed soups (see the tips starting on page 185 for instructions).

MORE TIPS FOR EASING INTO COOKING

FIVE INGREDIENT BACHELOR. Check out cookbooks featuring five ingredients or fewer, or with keywords in the title like "college student" or "bachelor." Just because you don't fit the demographic doesn't mean the food won't taste good to you.

§ **PAY ATTENTION** to the recipes on the back of the boxes or jars of the things you already have. Or visit websites like www. backofthebox.com/recipes.html.

§ **WATCH** *FOOD NETWORK* **SHOWS** like *Semi-Homemade with Sandra Lee* that focus on using simple store-bought ingredients in time-saving, creative ways.

§ **TREAT YOUR FREEZER AS AN EXTENSION OF YOUR PANTRY.** Keep it stocked with frozen dinners that help prevent takeout temptation.

MAKE IT FUN

Meal assembly stations are popping up all over the country in response to the everyday chef's hectic lifestyle. These facilities do all the prep work like chopping, slicing, and dicing for you. You show up with a group of friends and make a night of it. When you're done, you leave with meals that are ready to go. While it does cost more than if you were to make the same thing at home, these meals typically cost less than restaurant fare—plus you may be inspired to try some new recipes at home later on.

For a listing of meal assembly retailers in your area, visit this website: www.mealassembly.net.

Step Down to Savings

In your pursuit for frugality, trying to do too much too soon is almost certain to lead to failure. Just as a dieter is sure to fall off the wagon by implementing too many lifestyle changes at once, the same goes for your food habits. Trying the things that are easy for you to change without feeling deprived will help ensure your success.

Going from sit-down restaurants to cooking at home is quite a leap. Try making small changes slowly so you can get used to the new lifestyle. Once you feel comfortable with those changes, move on to the next step. You'll be inspired by your success (as well as the money you save!). It's a "Step Down to Savings" approach.

STEP ONE

Still frequent your favorite restaurants, but instead of eating there, take your dinner to go. If nothing else, that saves you the cost of the 15 to 20 percent tip. Plus, you get used to eating dinner at your own dinner table. Most restaurant entrées are too big for one meal. When you eat in a restaurant, the food that is left on the plate is just thrown away. If you bring the meal home, you can stick the leftovers into the fridge to enjoy later. And you already have the to-go container for storage!

STEP TWO

Instead of getting your food to go from a restaurant, try going to the supermarket and get your dinner from the deli section. Many high-end grocery stores now have all sorts of prepared dishes available from chicken to ribs, from sushi to designer salads. While you're in the grocery store, you might like to pick up a couple of items to pack for breakfast—a bottled juice, a yogurt, a piece of fruit, and a breakfast pastry—pretty much what you may be already eating but paying two or three times as much for in a company cafeteria. That way breakfast will be waiting for you in the refrigerator and you can just grab it and go.

STEP THREE

Recognize how easy some of those restaurant and deli meals are to prepare at home. Why buy a cooked steak at a restaurant when a quick trip to the grocery store would get the same steak, which could be grilled on the barbecue? The benefit is you get to enjoy fresher food and more time at home.

—TIPS COURTESY OF CATHERINE HEPNER, EAGLE, IDAHO

FOOD AWAY FROM HOME

In 1955, families spent about 25 percent of their food budget on meals prepared away from home. Today that number has nearly doubled to 48 percent. While it's probably unrealistic to give up eating out completely, changing your restaurant habits just a little can take a big bite out of your overall food budget.

Cut Back on the Restaurant Habit

For many, visiting a restaurant is a luxury that goes beyond simply providing something to eat. Bonding with family in a stress-free environment without prep and cleanup is a big draw: It's no wonder that the National Restaurant Association found that 69 percent of adults said that purchasing meals from restaurants, take-out, and delivery places makes it easier for families with children to manage their day-to-day lives. Here are some ways to trim your restaurant budget, relax with friends and family, and save money at the same time.

START A POTLUCK GROUP. Once a month, have friends over for a potluck dinner. Keep things easy and simple for everyone. Use paper plates and napkins, and insist on no-pressure recipes. Focus on a simple night with friends and you'll get the social interaction you crave without spending a lot of money. Assign each household a different category such as salad, dessert, or appetizer to avoid getting too much of one thing. Don't be afraid to ask guests to BYOB as well.

DATE NIGHTS AT HOME. Creating a special dinner at home has a couple of distinct advantages over going out: You spend less on the food, and you don't have to pay a babysitter! Put the kids to bed and enjoy a special late-night meal with your spouse. Pick something easy like crab legs and melted butter. It doesn't take much time to prepare and costs much less than ordering the same thing in a restaurant. Set the mood by using table linens and candles as well as turning on some of your favorite music. See page 249 for even more ideas!

HOUSEPARTY.COM. When you apply and are accepted as a house-party.com VIP, a sponsor such as Domino's Pizza or Bumblebee Tuna will provide the food and everything necessary for you to throw a party within your own home for free. In exchange, you agree to spread the word about their products with the people you invite as well as by sharing online feedback.

$ **TRACK SPENDING AND SET A BUDGET FOR DINING OUT.** Chances are you'd be surprised how much you spend on meals eaten away from home. For one month, track every fast food, convenience store, vending machine, and restaurant purchase your family makes. In most cases, the total will surprise you. Next, figure out what your budget can realistically handle and make it a goal to stick to that amount next month.

$ **ONLY PAY CASH.** Studies show that people are willing to spend more at retail establishments when paying with plastic, whether the plastic is a debit, credit, or gift card. Bring cash only when you do dine out, which makes the financial outlay more tangible to you.

$ **SET CONDITIONS FOR NIGHTS OUT.** Make eating out special by setting conditions for your family. Some families instill a twenty-four-hour waiting period before going to restaurants to avoid using them for the sake of convenience only. Other families will only eat out on "kids eat free" nights. Set the conditions that make sense for your family (and your budget).

TAKE ADVANTAGE OF RESTAURANT DISCOUNTS

You don't have to give up going to restaurants entirely to save money; you simply have to find ways to eat out for less. Learning the ins and outs of when to eat and where to find the best bargains can help.

$ **GO ON "KIDS EAT FREE" NIGHTS.** Instead of heading to your favorite restaurant on the weekend, eat out during the week when there are more specials such as happy hours and "kids eat free" nights, which are typically Monday or Tuesday.

USE RESTAURANT LOYALTY PROGRAMS AND BIRTHDAY CLUBS. Diners of any age can sign up for restaurant loyalty programs and birthday clubs to maximize savings at the places they frequent regularly. For example, T.G.I. Friday's gives you a coupon for a free appetizer after you join its Give Me More Stripes Club. Look for signup cards when you receive your bill, or sign up online. For a listing of "kids eat free" nights as well as loyalty clubs, birthday clubs, and other promotions, visit the Mommysavers Freebie Forums at http://mommysavers.com/boards/samples-freebies-offers/.

TRY A PRACTICE NIGHT. Is a new restaurant about to open in your community? Give it a call and ask the manager if they're hosting a trial run night. In most cases these events are reserved for friends, family, and business associates, but often the restaurant is available to accommodate additional diners as well.

SAVE WITH SECRET SHOPPING. An easy way to get a free meal is to sign up as a mystery shopper in your area. Shoppers dine in preselected restaurants for free in exchange for a report on the restaurant's services. Sometimes the shopper also receives a small payment for the report.

$ **LOOK FOR COUPONS.** You'll often find valuable coupons for restaurants in the Sunday coupon inserts, but they're also online. Check out the websites of your favorite restaurants as well as coupon sites like coupons.com. Mommysavers.com lists printable restaurant coupons in its deals and shopping forum, at http://mommysavers.com/boards/deals-shopping. Keep these coupons somewhere that you'll have access to when you're out, such as the glove compartment of your car or a coupon envelope in your purse. If they're stuck to your refrigerator with a magnet in your house, you're out of luck.

$ **CHECK YOUR REGISTER RECEIPTS FOR DISCOUNTS AND OFFERS.**

"Watch the bottom of your fast-food receipts. Sonic gives out redemption codes for free Route 44 drinks if you complete a quick two–three minute telephone survey."

—STACIA SEAGROVES, TOMBALL, TEXAS

$ **RESTAURANT WEEKS IN LOCAL CITIES.** Most major U.S. cities hold restaurant weeks that encourage people to come out and dine in participating restaurants at reduced rates. It's a way for the restaurants to get people in the door and sample what they have to offer as well as offer consumers a bargain. If your city offers one, be sure to sign up for their mailing list so you'll be the first to hear about participants and make early reservations.

RESTAURANT SITES THAT SAVE

With an Internet connection and a few minutes to browse, you can find places to dine at bargain prices. Noteworthy sites include:

RESTAURANT.COM. Look for coupons at the beginning of the month and the deepest price cuts at the end of the month. Cut your budget back by just $25 a week and you've saved $1,300 per year

ENTERTAINMENT.COM. Entertainment books cost about $25 to $35 but are well worth it if you're a frequent diner. They contain many dining coupons, including two-for-ones, dollars off a purchase, or free appetizers. Visit the Entertainment.com site to get a preview of the discounts available in your area. New books come out in September and get marked down throughout the course of the year. You may be able to get a second book at a greatly reduced price in the spring or summer. If you're going on a vacation, it often pays to purchase a book for the area you're visiting. Not only will you find coupons on restaurants, but you'll also get discounts on amusement parks, hotels, and other attractions.

CARDAVENUE.COM. Consumers can safely and securely buy, sell, and trade their pre-owned restaurant gift cards for a small fee. Look for cards to your favorite chain restaurants.

DINNERBROKER.COM. Rewards diners for making reservations during off-peak hours. Discounts range from 10 to 30 percent of the meal price. In addition to reservations, participating restaurants extend a variety of special offers to consumers ranging from free valet parking to prix fixe menus. Discounted gift certificates from participating restaurants are also available.

OPENTABLE.COM. OpenTable members can earn Dining Rewards Points for making and keeping reservations online. Once members have accumulated at least 2,000 points, they can be redeemed for OpenTable Dining Cheques.

LIFETAKESVISA.COM. If you're a Visa card holder, visit the "food and drink" section of this website. You'll see discounts and offers for national chain restaurants, including printable coupons

REWARDSNETWORK.COM. Earn free airline miles or cash rewards when you join, register your credit card, and eat at participating restaurants. It's free to join, but receiving cash back requires a $49 fee.

MONEYMAILER.COM. Lists local restaurant coupons by zip code or state.

EVEN MORE WAYS TO SAVE AT RESTAURANTS

DINE AT OFF-PEAK TIMES to get the best discounts, specials, and big savings. By choosing to eat out for lunch instead of dinner, you'll automatically save. Most lunch menus offer many of the same dinner options but at much smaller prices.

FILL UP ON FREEBIES. When ordering, take into consideration freebies like bread, tortilla chips, and munchies brought to you before the meal begins. Often, after eating them, you're satisfied, allowing you to split a meal or order a smaller portion.

$ **SODAS AND ALCOHOLIC BEVERAGES CAN RUIN YOUR RESTAURANT BUDGET.** Order a glass of water with a twist of lemon instead. If you're dining in at fast-food restaurants and want to order soda, always order the smallest size fountain drink and refill as needed.

$ **NOT EVERYONE NEEDS HIS OR HER OWN ENTRÉE.** When dining with your family, order a couple of entrées to share family-style, and fill in with low-cost side dishes or appetizers. To make the meal even healthier, order a side of steamed veggies. Or, instead of ordering two kids' meals, have the kids split an adult-size entrée.

$ **GET A DOGGIE BAG.** Restaurant portions are generally much larger than a normal-size meal. Fight the urge to consume the extra calories by cutting your meal in half when it arrives and saving the remainder for lunch the next day.

$ **SKIP THE TIP.** By all means don't slight your waitstaff, but instead look for places where tipping isn't necessary. Panera, Chipotle, BW3, and other chains where you place your order and pick up your food at the counter can help save you some cash on a tip.

$ **IF YOU LIVE IN A COLLEGE COMMUNITY, LOOK FOR RESTAURANTS NEAR CAMPUS.** College students don't typically have a lot of cash to spend on eating out, so the most successful restaurants in those areas are typically budget-friendly.

$ **OPT FOR A NO-FRILLS ESTABLISHMENT.** You'll pay for the fancy atmosphere and décor, so by opting for a no-frills mom-and-pop place, you can often find great food at terrific prices.

$ **CONSIDER MENU DESIGN PSYCHOLOGY.** Restaurants like to draw attention to their most profitable items by using bold type or placing them in spots where they're most likely to get noticed—usually at the top or bottom of the menu category. Have you noticed when most restaurants list their pricing, it's not in column form so it doesn't stand out? Restaurants also avoid putting a dollar sign near prices to avoid reminding patrons that they're spending money.

"When my husband and I eat out, we try to go during lunch rather than dinner, when meals are cheaper. I always find coupons in the Sunday paper (for example, last time we saved $4 at Olive Garden), and we save even more money by only drinking ice water with lemon. When we eat out as a whole family, we try to go to places that offer a discount such as kids eat for free night."

—DEANN LAGRANGE, CEDAR RAPIDS, IOWA

INEXPENSIVE DATE NIGHT THEMES FOR HOME-COOKED MEALS

It isn't hard to save money when cooking a romantic meal for two. Food prepared at home often costs less than a third of what it would in a restaurant, allowing you to splurge a little and still come in under $20 per meal.

But remember, your success doesn't lie with the money you spend or the food you serve—it's the memories you create. Setting the mood and doing something special outside of your normal routine is key.

PICNIC UNDER THE STARS. Throw a picnic blanket on the floor and enjoy an evening under the (faux) stars. Pack a basket of finger foods such as specialty cheeses, crackers, and fresh fruits. If you have a heartier appetite, try pita sandwiches paired with pasta or potato salad. CD sounds of crickets chirping as well as glow-in-the-dark stars on the ceiling help bring the outside in.

AN EVENING IN PARIS. Bring Parisian romance under the Eiffel Tower to your own home for an upscale, romantic experience. Try a classic French meal such as coq au vin or beef Bourguignon followed by a rich, decadent dessert like French chocolate mousse. Get out the candles, fine china, and tablecloth (if you don't have one, a flat bedsheet works just as well). Dress as if you were at a fancy restaurant—no slippers or sweats allowed!

FOR LOBSTER LOVERS. Seafood lovers will enjoy creating an oceanside eatery in their own dining room. Even with grocery prices on the rise, Maine lobster may be the best deal out there for frugal foodies. A drop in demand, combined with an above-average supply, has resulted in terrific prices. With lobster prices as low as $6.99 a pound, you'll be able to afford great sides like steamed broccoli and a baked potato. Look for a CD of ocean sounds at your local dollar store.

BEACH GETAWAY. A casual meal on the beach can create warm feelings on a cold winter night. Try grilled fish tacos or a shrimp cocktail and some fresh fruit with a blended margarita (don't forget the umbrella stirrers) to get your tropical groove on. Try Pandora.com for some free Latin beats.

SKI LODGE. Snuggle up on a warm fluffy blanket while you watch the snowflakes drift to the ground. Comfort foods like beef stew or slow-cooker chili paired with hot, home-made crusty bread are sure to add to the cozy vibe. Finish it off with a warm nightcap such as hot buttered rum, mulled wine, or hot cider. Even if you don't have a fireplace, you can create a lodge atmosphere for free. Simply search "virtual fireplace" on YouTube and play one of the many videos on your computer screen.

CAMP IN. Light a fire in the fireplace as you "camp out" indoors. Prepare steaks, hamburgers, or hot dogs on the grill, paired with ice cold beer and s'mores for dessert. Hit your dollar store for CD sounds of wolves howling and evergreen-scented candles to remind you of the great outdoors.

ITALIAN FEAST. Turn your home into a cozy Italian bistro with the sounds of Pavarotti and great smells emanating from the kitchen. Fettuccine with marinara sauce is an inexpensive dinner option. Because it's a meatless main dish, you'll have money left over for homemade breadsticks (use your bread machine for the dough), fresh Parmesan cheese, and a bottle of wine. Perfect the art of plating the meal for maximum visual impact. Wipe sauce spots off around the rim of the plates and garnish the meal with parsley or fresh basil.

$ **DINNER AND A MOVIE.** Dim the lights and draw the curtains to create the atmosphere of an old-fashioned cinema right in your own home. Pick a romantic classic from your library's DVD collection to watch with your meal. Plan your dinner around the movie's theme. For example, try pairing the movie *Titanic* with lamb and mint sauce—straight from the ill-fated ship's actual menu. Don't forget the popcorn and cinema candy classics like Good 'N Plenty and Junior Mints.

$ **RETRO ROMANCE.** A 1970s retro theme is perfect for a fun, casual dinner. Fondue is definitely a departure from the normal cooking routine. Try dipping bread cubes in your choice of cheeses: Gruyère, cheddar, or Swiss. Or dip fruits like apples, bananas, or pears in a rich chocolate or butterscotch sauce. Place the dinner table in a different location in your home so you feel like you're breaking from routine.

"I have ALWAYS loved a good steak dinner at Texas Roadhouse. I could never figure out how they get their steak so tender, juicy, and flavorful. But I finally figured out their simple secret! The steakhouses use a dry rub. It's very simple. For a basic rub, I use equal parts of garlic powder, paprika, and seasoned salt. I generously rub the seasoning into the meat, cover it, and put it back into the fridge for at least an hour before grilling. Simple! You could easily pay $40 at a steakhouse for two nice Delmonico steak dinners. I buy two steaks for about $10 on sale at the grocery store. Add a couple baked potatoes and a nice green salad, and you have yourself a nice steakhouse dinner for a fraction of the price!"

—BEKAH NOVITZKE, HARRISBURG, PENNSYLVANIA

INTERNET SITES CAN HELP YOU FIND COPYCAT RECIPES FOR RESTAURANT FOODS YOU LOVE. Entering terms like this in your search engine will almost always yield many recipes:

- restaurant + name of the food + recipe

For example, entering "Red Lobster Cheddar Bay Biscuits Recipe" in the Google search field produces over 18,000 results.

FAMILY FOODS: FEEDING THE LITTLE ONES AFFORDABLY

Feeding the smallest members of your family can add up to a big expense, but it doesn't have to be that way. From baby to beyond, here are some ways to make meals special, nutritious, and inexpensive.

Baby, Baby!

$ **IF YOU USE INFANT FORMULA, JOIN THE MANUFACTURER'S MAILING LISTS** to receive valuable offers by mail. Not only will you receive free samples, but you will also get coupons and retail checks good to purchase full cans of formula. Try these sites:

  $ http://similac.com
  $ www.enfamil.com
  $ www.gerber.com
  $ www.parentschoiceformula.com

OTHER WAYS TO SAVE ON FORMULA

$ **BUY THE STORE BRAND.** By law, all formula manufacturers have to adhere to the same FDA guidelines. So, by purchasing a cheaper brand, you don't have to worry that you're skimping on nutrition.

$ **PRICES FOR FORMULA MAY VARY WITHIN THE SAME CHAIN.** For example, one discount retailer may sell its Similac for one price while another store 20 miles away sells it for a bit more. Be sure to check all stores (or better yet, call) in your area to compare prices.

$ **ASK YOUR PEDIATRICIAN FOR FORMULA SAMPLES** when you're there for your well-baby checkup. Most offices have an abundance of samples and are happy to share them with you if you ask.

$ **GO ONLINE.** Amazon.com is another not-so-well-known source for baby formula. They offer the large economy-size cans, often at prices less than Target's or Walmart's. As an added bonus, they often offer free shipping on qualifying orders.

$ **INVESTIGATE INSURANCE COVERAGE.** If your baby needs a specialized formula for medical reasons such as reflux or allergies, you can try to get your insurance provider to cover the cost. Prescriptions can be written for formulas; be sure to ask your doctor for details.

$ **SIGN UP FOR SAVINGS.** Parents and parents-to-be can sign up for their supermarket's baby clubs to get store discounts and special offers. Redeem your formula checks and other baby coupons at supermarkets that offer baby bucks. In most cases you will get the full value of item in baby bucks and still receive your coupon discount.

BARGAIN BABY FOOD

Cereal

§ **CREAM OF WHEAT IS AN ACCEPTABLE SUBSTITUTE FOR BABY CEREAL.** Like baby cereal, it is also fortified with vitamins and iron. It is available in bulk at restaurant/bakery supply stores and warehouse stores like Sam's Club, BJ's, and Costco.

§ **INSTANT OATS PULVERIZED IN A BLENDER MAKE AN INSTANT BABY CEREAL.** You can purchase the oats in bulk. Prepare it ahead of time and store it in an airtight container. When you're ready to use it, just mix with breast milk, formula, or water.

§ **MAKE YOUR OWN RICE CEREAL.** Start with ½ cup brown rice, pulverizing it in your blender. Bring 2 cups water to a boil. Reduce heat and add rice. Stir briskly, and remove from the burner. Cover and let stand for ten minutes, stirring occasionally to prevent sticking and clumping.

Do-It-Yourself Baby Food

§ **MAKE YOUR OWN BABY FOOD.** This can be as simple as steaming veggies until soft and pureeing to the desired consistency. Cook your vegetables, meat, and fruit, then put them in a blender or food processor and blend well. Spoon into ice cube trays to freeze. Empty the ice cubes into freezer bags and thaw as needed for each serving. One cube is equivalent to one small serving; two is equivalent to one large serving. Or plop spoonfuls onto a sheet of wax paper on a cookie sheet and freeze.

CHOP YOUR LEFTOVERS. When your baby starts to eat table food, puree or chop up your leftovers, put them in baby food jars, and freeze. Be sure to mark the date on the jar. If you add a lot of seasoning to your foods, be sure to make baby's serving first and leave the spices out.

BOILED POTATO BOOST. If your baby is partial to that thick, smooth, congealed texture that baby food is famous for, add a little bit of boiled potato to his food when you puree it.

DON'T BUY JUICES FOR YOUR BABY IN THE BABY FOOD AISLE. Instead, make your own using regular juice and adding water. Juices for babies are really just regular juice with a higher water concentration and a little vitamin C added. Your baby should be getting a sufficient supply of vitamin C in breast milk or formula already. Mix about ½ cup water to ½ cup juice. Avoid juices like orange juice, which may upset little tummies, and apple cider, which is unpasteurized.

BABY FOOD IN THE ADULT AISLE. If you don't have enough time to make your own baby food, buy foods marketed to adults that work for baby. Unsweetened applesauce, for example, works well for baby because it is the same consistency as baby food. Peel a ripe banana and spoon-feed it to baby. This costs much less than a jar of baby food and is virtually the same thing!

SWITCH TO TABLE FOOD

Make the switch to table food early rather than relying on jarred baby food. Gradually add more and more texture to your baby's diet, so that by seven or eight months, your baby will be able to eat bite-size pieces of avocado, peas, cooked carrots, and so forth. He will also have lots of fun feeding himself!

Make your own "stage two" foods for babies ready to self-feed instead of buying expensive jarred foods. Buy cottage cheese (large-curd works best) and rinse in a colander. The pieces that remain are great for self-feeders, and cost much less than food specifically packaged for babies and toddlers. Other great foods for babies ready to self-feed include berries (cut into small pieces), cooked carrots, Cheerios, egg yolks (skip the whites until baby is one year old), fish, green beans, graham crackers, noodles, pears, peas, sweet potatoes, squash, rice, and rice cakes. Remember to cook vegetables thoroughly so they're soft.

Prepare cereal with very little liquid so that it has a thick, clumpy consistency. Babies that are learning to self-feed can use their fingers to pick it up.

Remember, foods that are unsafe for baby include peanuts and other nuts, popcorn, hot dogs, sausages, grapes, apple chunks, raw carrots, peanut butter, and other hard meats.

Moving On…Big-Kid Food for Less

Big kids have special tastes and requests when it comes to the food they eat, and food manufacturers know this. Grocery products marketed specifically to kids make up a $1.6 billion business. Here are just a few ways to make the foods kids enjoy affordably as well as to introduce kids to smart shopping practices.

SHOPPING WITH KIDS

Since impulse purchases can ruin any grocery budget, it may be easier and more efficient to shop alone and leave the kids at home. However, that's not always a possibility. Here are some ways to make the most of your grocery trips with the kids, teach them about money, and avoid unnecessary purchases.

- **INVOLVE KIDS WITH MEAL PLANNING** before you even set foot in the store. Ask them which healthy foods and snacks they're hungry for and add them to your shopping list. Allow older kids to plan an entire meal, complete with main course and sides.

- **IF A PARENT MUST SHOP WITH KIDS, LET IT BE MOM.** According to sociologist Paco Underhill, men are more likely to give in to children's requests for impulse items.

- **FEED 'EM UP.** Make sure your children are well-fed before bringing them to the store.

- **FREE COOKIES!** Many grocery store bakery departments offer free cookies to little ones shopping with their parents. Munching on something sweet often takes their minds off other treats and temptations.

- **PLAY I-SPY.** It's a great way to teach kids to recognize certain fruits, vegetables, and foods they're not yet familiar with. Plus, it provides a fun distraction for them while keeping your focus on reading labels, comparing prices, and finding the best deals.

Another variation: have them look for things that begin with a certain letter.

TEAR OFF A SMALL PORTION OF YOUR LIST AND HAVE OLDER CHILDREN HELP FIND THE ITEMS ON IT. Challenge them to look for the best deals, a great way to get them started on the path to making good financial decisions.

GIVE EACH CHILD $1 TO SPEND ON SOMETHING IN THE GROCERY STORE. You set the guidelines: It could range from something new in the produce section to a candy bar at the checkout lane.

HAVE YOUR CHILD SELECT SOMETHING TO DONATE TO A LOCAL FOOD PANTRY EACH TIME YOU VISIT THE STORE. It's a great opportunity to reinforce the concept of giving to those less fortunate.

CLIP COUPONS. Get kids into the coupon game. If your children are old enough, have them clip and organize your coupons for you. Apply your coupon savings toward something the kids and the rest of the family can enjoy together (such as a day at a theme park, a new game, or a meal at a favorite restaurant). Save the money in a glass jar so that the kids can watch the money add up.

Kids and Cooking

Getting kids into healthy routines at a young age can sometimes be a challenge. Here are some helpful hints to get them not only to accept the foods you're making, but to feel like they're contributing to the family meal as well.

$ **LET THEM HELP.** The more involved kids are in the preparation of your meals, the more likely they are to try something. Make it fun for them! This gnocchi recipe is fun for preschoolers because of its play dough–like consistency. Have your little one roll the dough out like a snake and then cut little tiny pieces off with a plastic knife (make sure it's one that's appropriate for a child to use).

Simple Gnocchi

- 1 cup dry potato flakes
- 1 cup boiling water
- 1 egg, beaten
- 1 teaspoon salt
- 1 teaspoon ground ginger
- 1½ cups all-purpose flour

Combine potato flakes and boiling water. Allow to cool. Add in remaining ingredients and mix until dough forms. Roll out dough like a snake and cut into small, bite-size pieces. Drop into boiling water. When dumplings rise and start to float, remove with slotted spoon. Serve with any meat or pasta sauce.

$ **DIP IT OR DISGUISE IT.** Sneaky moms have all sorts of tricks to get young kids to eat fruits and vegetables. Dipping in sauces is one. Raw veggies go great with ranch sauce, cooked veggies with cheese. Another theory is that kids won't balk about eating it if they don't know it's there. Cauliflower puree can be snuck into mashed potatoes, zucchini can be incorporated into breads and muffins, and other veggies are hidden well in soups, stews, and sauces.

§ **IT'S IN THE PRESENTATION.** For kids, packaging is important. Instead of juice boxes or pouches, invest in cute refillable water bottles that can be taken on the go. Reuse Lunchables containers by making your own contents to go inside, and then use a press-and-seal plastic wrap and adorn with a few stickers.

§ **STUFF FOR SMALL FOLKS CARRIES A BIG PRICE TAG.** When you do buy grocery products marketed just for kids, such as cotton candy-flavored yogurt and noodles shaped like cartoon characters, be sure to compare the price per ounce. Many come in packages that are smaller than their standard non-kid counterparts, so while the price of the product may be the same, the price per ounce is quite different.

Product	Price Per Ounce
Yoplait Kids Yogurt	$0.153
Yoplait Original Yogurt	$0.125
Ore-Ida ABC Tater Tots	$0.162
Ore-Ida Original Tater Tots	$0.116
Scooby-Doo Mac and Cheese (Kraft)	$0.235
Original Mac and Cheese (Kraft)	$0.103

§ **PLAY RESTAURANT.** Playing restaurant is a great way to get young cooks as well as their younger siblings involved with meal preparation in a fun, creative way. Have the older child prepare a basic menu, complete with beverages, side dishes, a main course, and dessert selections. One parent can assist ın the kitchen while the other parent plays customer. Younger siblings can get in the game too by playing waiter or waitress. Of course chefs' hats and aprons help the "game," too!

BE PERSISTENT. It's only natural to gravitate toward favorite meals and dishes that are easy to prepare. Don't get stuck in a rut!

THE FRUGAL LUNCHBOX

The average school lunch in America costs only $1.80—a challenge for today's mom to beat in both price and convenience. However, a little organization is all you'll need to send your kids to school with nutritious lunches while saving money at the same time. By using some of these ideas you can get the average price per lunch under $0.75, which means with more than one child in school, you could save hundreds each year.

DIVVY IT UP. Prepackaged items can take a big bite out of your budget. Instead, buy a box of 100-count sandwich bags and divide big bags of pretzels, popcorn, chips, or other snacks into individual-size portions yourself—or better yet, have the kids do it. Separate individual servings of applesauce, pudding, carrot sticks, or other healthy foods your child will eat into reusable containers. Taking just a few minutes at the start of each week on a regular basis can add up to big savings over the course of the year.

CONSIDER THE PACKAGING. Today's toss-away containers can be expensive—not to mention bad for the environment. Use reusable containers and utensils instead, from cloth napkins to "real" forks and spoons, right down to the lunchbox itself, which will pay for itself over time in comparison with brown paper sacks. You don't have to purchase special containers: leftover yogurt containers with lids and margarine tubs serve the purpose well. Don't forget to invest in a good thermos, too. It's not just for milk: Use it to keep soups, pasta dishes, or last night's leftovers warm. Keep drinks cold by freezing a small portion overnight. Fill your container with the remaining portion in the morning.

SAVE ON SCHOOL LUNCHES. You don't have to pay full price for your child's lunchbox, either. Choose an insulated box or bag to help keep hot foods hot and cold foods cold. Great deals can be found if you wait to buy until late September, when back-to-school gear hits the clearance rack. Or buy a used one at a thrift store or garage sale. Don't worry about the artwork; take it off with fingernail polish remover and use stickers to embellish it with your child's favorite characters.

BE SANDWICH-SAVVY. Chicken, tuna, and egg salad sandwiches are more economical than sandwich meats. An insulated bag with a freezer pack will keep them cold until lunchtime. Make your own freezer pack by freezing a juice box or reusable drink container with ice water.

$ **MAKE LUNCH FUN AGAIN.** Use cookie cutters to create fun sandwich shapes. You can also experiment with different breads such as pita pockets and bakery rolls. Tortillas are great for wrap sandwiches and making tortilla pinwheels with meat and cheese as well. Throw in condiment packets left over from fast-food trips.

$ **ONLY PACK WHAT THEY'LL EAT.** Don't pack more than your child can eat. If he's tossing a big portion away because he's too full or doesn't like it, you're throwing your money away. Involve your children in the selection and preparation process as much as you can to ensure that food ends up in their stomachs—and not the trash can.

$ **FREEZE IT FOR TIME SAVINGS.** A lot of brown-bag staples can be prepared ahead of time and frozen, saving time and money. Additionally, they'll help keep things cool in the morning and will thaw by lunchtime. Among them:

- $ ½ cup each fruit cocktail, sour cream, and whipped topping for a sweet dessert
- $ Homemade yogurt (page 191) with mix-ins like granola or preserves
- $ Tortilla pinwheels made with cream cheese, shredded cheddar, and lunchmeat rolled and sliced
- $ Pasta salad with chunks of cheese and meats like pepperoni or ham

$ **THE LAST WORD.** Before you brown-bag it, consider the cost. School lunches are actually a pretty good value—and you can't beat them for convenience. Your kids get a nutritious, hot meal—

and you save the work of packing it. Additionally, most public schools also offer free or reduced prices to families that qualify.

Great Family Meals on a Budget

In today's hustle-and-bustle world, it's more important than ever to serve family meals at the table. This means no eating in front of the TV or running through the drive-thru. Use the time to reconnect as a family and talk about your day. In fact, University of Minnesota Project Eating Among Teens II (Project EAT) researchers found that children from families who take time for eating together are less likely to develop eating disorders, be overweight, or engage in risky behavior such as drinking, drugs, smoking, or sex. Here are some easy tips to make it happen:

- **FORMAL NIGHT.** At a minimum, make at least one night a week a formal family dinner around the dining room table, but aim for five meals eaten together in all. Picking the same night each week enhances the experience.

- **FAMILY MEALS DON'T NECESSARILY HAVE TO BE DINNER.** If eating together at breakfast or lunch is easier, that's fine, too.

- **30-MINUTE MINIMUM.** Try to stay at the table for a minimum of half an hour.

- **HAVE SOME CONVERSATION STARTERS HANDY.** Suggestions include:
    - What made you laugh today?
    - Did someone do something nice for you?
    - What was your proudest moment of the day?

- **ASSIGN CHILDREN REGULAR TASKS** such as setting and clearing the table, or loading the dishwasher.

- **AVOID ARGUING OR NEGATIVE TALK DURING DINNER.** It should be a relaxed family experience free from negativity.

- **DON'T STRESS OVER CREATING A THREE-COURSE HOMEMADE MEAL.** Do what's easiest for you to make it happen. It's not the food that's served that's important, it's the ritual itself.

Smart Snacks

Getting kids off overly processed snacks and foods isn't always easy. Here are some ideas to make snacking satisfying, frugal, and fun.

- **BUY IN BULK AND DIVIDE.** Instead of buying those handy snack packs of chips, buy a large bag and separate them in plastic bags in individual serving sizes. Pudding, applesauce, and yogurt can also be purchased in large containers and separated into individual-size cups.

- **LOOK FOR PREPACKAGED SNACK BARGAINS** at bakery outlets and dollar stores.

- **LEARN TO MAKE YOUR OWN COOKIES,** cereal bars, and chips. Not only will you save money, but you'll also be doing your health a favor. Homemade versions contain more wholesome ingredients and fewer preservatives.

FILL UP ON HEALTHY SNACKS. Eat fresh fruits and veggies and whole grains as much as possible. To make them more exciting, prepare them in a fun way. Some ideas include:

- Kabobs made with any combination of cheese, fruit, vegetables, and sliced or cubed cooked meat (remove the skewers before serving).
- Frozen fruit cubes (freeze pureed applesauce, crushed peaches or pears, fruit juice, or any fruit into cubes) or popsicles
- Gelatin blocks or "wigglers" with canned or fresh fruit
- Fresh vegetables with ranch sauce or hummus (on next page)
- Yogurt topped with fresh fruit or nuts
- Orange creamsicles made from orange juice and plain yogurt
- Yogurt dip with bananas
- Fruit smoothies (blend milk with bananas, peaches, or frozen strawberries and add a dash of cinnamon and sugar)
- Bagels with various soft cream spreads
- Quick breads or muffins made with carrots, zucchini, pumpkin, bananas, dates, or squash

PICK HEARTY PROTEINS. Instead of typical snack foods, opt for healthy proteins such as hard-boiled eggs, low-fat cheeses, or a mini-meal such as:

- Flour or corn tortillas with refried beans and canned chili, sprinkled with grated cheese, and topped with yogurt or sour cream
- Potato skins sprinkled with shredded cheese, broiled and topped with either yogurt or sour cream

- English muffins or pita bread topped with spaghetti sauce, grated cheese, and lean cuts of turkey or other lean meats, broiled or baked and cut into fourths
- Pita bread with lean sliced meat such as chicken or turkey, cheese, lettuce, and tomato in an open pocket

Hummus

1 15-ounce can chickpeas, rinsed and drained; reserve ½ cup liquid

¼ cup tahini

¼ cup lemon juice

3 tablespoons extra virgin olive oil

2 cloves garlic, crushed

½ teaspoon cumin

¼ cup fresh cilantro leaves, finely chopped

Puree all ingredients using a stick blender or food processor. Variation: Omit cumin and cilantro and add ½ jar roasted red peppers.

DIY MICROWAVE POPCORN

Popcorn isn't just a frugal snack; it's good for you, too! It's a whole grain that's naturally high in fiber, and when prepared without butter or oil, it's practically fat-free. Did you know that you can make your very own microwave popcorn with a brown paper lunch sack? Simply put ¼ cup popcorn kernels into a brown paper bag and fold the top closed. Pop on your microwave's high setting for three to four minutes or until there are five seconds between pops.

TASTY VARIATIONS:

- Add grated Parmesan cheese and garlic powder as a topping.
- Before placing in the bag, coat the kernels with a tablespoon

of sugar and two teaspoons vegetable oil for delicious kettle corn.

DID YOU KNOW? Popcorn's popularity surged during the years of the Great Depression. At just $0.05 to $0.10 per bag, it was one of the only "luxuries" families could afford.

BAKED TORTILLA CRISPS

Create your own baked tortilla chips quickly and economically by starting with premade flour tortillas. Cut the tortillas in triangle-shaped wedges with a pizza cutter or scissors. Spritz with olive oil, dust with a dash of salt and/or garlic powder, and bake on a cookie sheet for ten to fifteen minutes at 350°F until lightly browned. For a sweet variation, dust with a cinnamon/sugar mixture and serve with homemade fruit salsa or yogurt dip.

VARIATION

Do the same thing with pita bread to make pita crisps.

CREATE FOOD TRADITIONS

Holidays and special occasions are reason for going out and celebrating, but sometimes creating your own special occasions at home is even more memorable, and almost always less expensive.

Holiday and Seasonal Traditions

- Heart-shaped pancakes on Valentine's Day
- Corned beef and cabbage on St. Patrick's Day

- Food pranks on April Fool's Day such as "disguising" Rice Krispies cereal as meatloaf
- Breakfast in bed on Mother's Day or Father's Day
- Watermelon seed-spitting contests
- Corn on the cob in the summer
- Turkey on Thanksgiving or Christmas

Non-Holiday Food Traditions

- **PRESERVING YOUR FAMILY'S ETHNIC HERITAGE** by learning to make meals your parents and grandparents made
- **HAVE A POPCORN AND MOVIE NIGHT ON THE WEEKENDS.** Buy popcorn in bulk and cook it on the stovetop for an even more special memory.
- **HOMEMADE PIZZA** is a great way to use up leftover veggies and meat. Make one night of the week pizza night.

> *"We try to make each family member's birthday extra special by holding cooking contests based on their favorite foods. Last year we had a chili cook-off on my dad's birthday. He loved it and we ended up with six different types of chili. Everyone shares leftovers, so we all got meals for the next day or two. We also did brownies for my brother's birthday one year, although those didn't render quite as many leftovers to take home!"*
>
> —TRUDY FLETCHER, EAST LIVERPOOL, OHIO

On the Go: Traveling and Vacations

It's always a challenge to save money while on vacation. When you're on the road, sometimes ease and convenience win over health consciousness. Try to balance the bad with the good if possible, and use some of these tricks to learn to avoid overspending on food.

It all starts with making sure you bring plenty of snacks for hungry travelers.

KEEP A FEW CANS OF SODA STORED IN YOUR CAR when the temperature isn't too hot or too cold (to avoid explosions). When you're making a drive-thru run, ask for a cup of ice and fill it with the soda you already have.

"If any of you have kids in sports like I do, you know how expensive it is to eat at their sporting events. We were spending up to $100 a weekend. Now I have started packing our food and drinks to take with us. I have a big bag that I use to take pop, water, juice boxes, and crackers along with us. I also make sandwiches with small dollar-size buns and pack them in a soft lunch box-type cooler along with some cheese sticks."

—SHERYL OSWEILIER, WASECA, MINNESOTA

$ **BRING ALONG HEALTHY OPTIONS.** Muffins, granola bars, dry cereal, and cheese sticks make easy and healthy snacks.

$ **PACK THE PEANUT BUTTER.** The makings for peanut butter sandwiches are inexpensive and easy to transport.

$ **CHOOSE SNACKS CAREFULLY.** Look for items that won't spoil, aren't too messy, and keep kids interested and even entertained (such as fruit leathers that leave tongue tattoos).

$ **BRING AN INSULATED COOLER** along so that you can curb your cravings without spending money unnecessarily at restaurants. Include the makings of your favorite sandwiches, cheese and meat sticks, fresh fruit, and other more filling treats.

$ **TRAIL MIXES** are great because they're not messy, are fairly healthy, and can be adjusted according to your taste. Include items such as

- $ Nuts such as peanuts or cashews
- $ Raisins, dried cranberries, or dried apricots
- $ Pretzels
- $ Dry cereal such as Cheerios or Chex
- $ Sunflower seeds
- $ M&M's or chocolate chips
- $ Candy corn
- $ Shredded coconut

BEYOND SNACKS

$ WEIGH THE COST OF A HOTEL THAT INCLUDES A CONTINENTAL BREAKFAST. Sometimes you'll save money doing this, especially if you have several hungry kids to feed. Make breakfast a big meal and go lighter on lunch and dinner.

$ BYOB (BRING YOUR OWN BREAKFAST). If a continental breakfast isn't included with your stay, be sure to pack breakfast bars, rolls, donuts, or even cereal and milk packed in a cooler.

$ INVESTIGATE RESTAURANT PROMOTIONS. Some hotel restaurants also offer a "kids eat free" promotion with each paying adult.

$ FIND A HOTEL THAT INCLUDES A MICROWAVE AND REFRIGERATOR. You'll be able to make snacks and light meals in your room. Pack snacks, beverages, and other foods ahead of time to avoid vending machine or mini-bar charges.

$ KITCHENETTE BONUS. If you have access to a kitchenette during your stay, pack an entire suitcase of food for snacks and meals. When you've used up the food, you'll be able to use the empty suitcase for souvenirs.

$ GET REWARDED WHILE YOU'RE AWAY FROM HOME. If you're a loyalty club shopper, shop at grocery stores within the same family of stores. For example, Jewel is in the same family of stores as Albertson's, and the loyalty card will work at both locations.

PACK WATER BOTTLES BEFORE YOU HEAD OUT FOR THE DAY.
Partially freeze them, adding water to the top before you head out. That way they'll stay cold all day.

DID YOU KNOW? You can bake slice-and-bake cookies on your dashboard in hot and sunny weather. As long as it's more than 95 degrees outside, this trick actually works. Park your car in full sun and place a cookie sheet of slice-and-bake cookie dough on the dashboard (place a towel underneath the cookie sheet to avoid damage to your dashboard). You'll need about two and a half hours to bake them completely, but be sure to check that they're done. Try it when you're visiting a museum, attending a ballgame, or visiting another attraction. Not only will you have a great snack, you'll have a great-smelling car and create some sweet memories in the process.

SHOWING KIDS HOW TO GIVE BACK: YOUR SAVINGS CAN HELP OTHERS

- **CONSIDER REINVESTING YOUR SAVINGS** to help an entrepreneurial family in a third-world country work their way out of poverty. Micro loans made through Kiva.org can help a woman in Africa who earns money selling vegetables and spices at a local market reinvest in her stock, or a fisherman in Asia buy new nets. Loans require as little as $25 and are paid back with interest. For more information, visit kiva.org.

- **THE BOX TOPS FOR EDUCATION PROGRAM** has helped raise over $250 million for schools over its twelve-year history. To read more about eligible products and how to donate, visit this link: www.boxtops4education.com.

AFTERWORD

At Mommysavers.com I make it my personal mission to help moms live well for less. It's my belief that by saving money on everyday expenses, you can focus your money, time, and resources on the things you value most. Hopefully you can apply what you've learned within this book to help improve the quality of the meals you put on the table while saving money at the same time.

For more information, updates, and to discuss these topics, be sure to visit Mommysavers.com and sign up for our forums. Our wonderful community of frugal moms is available 24/7 to answer your toughest questions on eating well for less as well as saving money in any other category.

APPENDIX A:
FOOD ASSISTANCE PROGRAMS AND CHARITIES

If you've tried all the money-saving tips here and still can't afford to put healthy meals on the table, there is still hope. Hundreds of assistance programs exist to help struggling families eat well. Here are just a few:

SNAP (Supplemental Nutrition Assistance Program)
As of October 2008, the Federal Food Stamp Program renamed itself SNAP in an effort to reflect its mission of making food more accessible to low-income families. Eligibility is determined on a state-by-state basis and is largely dependent on income.

www.fns.usda.gov/fsp

WIC (Women, Infants, and Children)
WIC is a federal program designed to give short-term nutritional assistance to low-income women who are pregnant, infants, and children up to five years of age. It is administered on the state level and participants must meet income eligibility requirements.

www.fns.usda.gov/wic

Angel Food Ministries

Angel Food Ministries has been helping provide food relief to struggling families since 1994. Today, it helps over 500,000 families each month. Recipients get a box containing $65 worth of food, estimated to last a family of four an entire week, for the nominal price of $30. No income restrictions exist.

www.angelfoodministries.com

There are even sites on the Internet devoted to menu plans based on the AFM meals. Among them:

www.hillbillyhousewife.com/angelfood

SHARE

SHARE (Self-Help and Resource Exchange) is a program where people can purchase a package of food staples (meat, fruit, vegetables) valued at $35 for $18 and two hours of community service. There are no eligibility guidelines or income requirements. Programs are divided by region.

SHARE Colorado:

http://sharecolorado.com

SHARE Iowa:

www.shareiowa.com

SHARE Pennsylvania (serving Pennsylvania, Delaware, New Jersey, Metro New York, and Maryland):

www.sharefoodprogram.org

SHARE Wisconsin:

www.sharewi.org

SHARE Programs are also available in certain parts of California, Indiana, Virginia, Florida, Tennessee, and Kentucky.

Freecycle

The Freecycle Network is a grassroots and entirely nonprofit movement of people who are giving (and getting) stuff for free in their own towns. Each local online group is moderated by a volunteer. Membership is free. While the assortment of what's available on Freecycle is as varied as its membership, chances are you can benefit from food and seasonal fruits and vegetables being given away during peak season.

www.freecycle.org

APPENDIX B:
INGREDIENT SUBSTITUTIONS

Avoid a trip to the store to buy a necessary ingredient. Save gas, save time.

Baking powder

For 1 teaspoon of baking powder, use ¼ teaspoon baking soda, ½ teaspoon cream of tartar, plus ¼ teaspoon cornstarch. Or ⅓ teaspoon baking soda and ½ teaspoon cream of tartar.

Breadcrumbs

Instead use crushed potato chips, cornflakes, or crackers.

Buttermilk or sour milk

For 1 cup buttermilk, add 1 tablespoon lemon juice and enough milk to equal 1 cup.

Use 1 cup plain yogurt in place of 1 cup buttermilk.

Brown sugar

Use 1 cup white sugar plus 2 tablespoons molasses.

Cornstarch

Instead of 1 teaspoon cornstarch add 2 teaspoons flour.

Corn syrup

Substitute 1 cup honey for 1 cup light corn syrup.

Cream, heavy

For 1 cup cream to use in baking, combine ¾ cup milk with ⅓ cup butter or margarine.

Cream, light or half-and-half

For 1 cup light cream, substitute 1 cup evaporated milk, undiluted.

Cream of tartar

Instead of 1 teaspoon cream or tartar, add 1 teaspoon white vinegar or lemon juice.

Egg yolks

For two yolks, instead use one whole egg.

Honey

For 1 cup honey, use ¾ cup maple syrup, molasses, or corn syrup plus ½ cup white sugar.

Milk, evaporated

For 1 cup evaporated milk, substitute 1 cup cream or half-and-half.

Milk, sweetened condensed

1 cup instant nonfat dry milk

⅔ cup white sugar

½ cup boiling water

3 tablespoons butter

Process in a blender until smooth.

Milk, whole

Use 1 cup skim milk and 2 tablespoons melted butter or margarine.

Molasses

Instead of molasses, substitute either honey, dark corn syrup, or maple syrup.

Ricotta cheese

Substitute cottage cheese in place of ricotta.

Sour cream

For 1 cup sour cream, substitute 1 cup plain yogurt.

Sugar

Use ¾ cup honey, molasses, or corn syrup in place of 1 cup sugar. Reduce the other liquid ingredients by 2 tablespoons each and add a pinch of baking soda to neutralize acidity.

Or replace with light brown sugar.

Tapioca

For 1 tablespoon tapioca, substitute 1½ tablespoons flour.

Tomato juice

Substitute ½ cup tomato sauce and ½ cup water for 1 cup tomato juice.

Tomato sauce

For 2 cups tomato sauce, use ¾ cup tomato paste plus 1 cup water.

Vanilla extract

As a vanilla extract substitute, use almond extract, rum, or amaretto

Worcestershire sauce

Substitute steak sauce in place of Worcerstershire sauce.

Yogurt

Replace with either sour cream, buttermilk, or blended cottage cheese.

APPENDIX C:
MEASUREMENT EQUIVALENCY CHARTS

Liquid Measures

1 gal = 4 qt = 8 pt = 16 c = 128 fl oz

½ gal = 2 qt = 4 pt = 8 c = 64 fl oz

¼ gal = 1 qt = 2 pt = 4 c = 32 fl oz

½ qt = 1 pt = 2 c = 16 fl oz

¼ qt = ½ pt = 1 c = 8 fl oz

Dry Measures

1 c = 16 Tbsp = 48 tsp = 250 ml

¾ c = 12 Tbsp = 36 tsp = 175 ml

⅔ c = 10 ⅔ Tbsp = 32 tsp = 150 ml

½ c = 8 Tbsp = 24 tsp = 125 ml

⅓ c = 5 ⅓ Tbsp = 16 tsp = 75 ml

¼ c = 4 Tbsp = 12 tsp = 50 ml

⅛ c = 2 Tbsp = 6 tsp = 30 ml

1 Tbsp = 3 tsp = 15 ml

Measuring Guide

3 teaspoons = 1 tablespoon

4 tablespoons = ¼ cup

5 tablespoons + 1 teaspoon = ⅓ cup

8 tablespoons = ½ cup

1 cup = ½ pint

2 cups = 1 pint

4 cups (2 pints) = 1 quart

4 quarts = 1 gallon

16 ounces = 1 pound

Dash or pinch = less than ⅛ teaspoon

Common Abbreviations

t = teaspoon

tsp = teaspoon

T = tablespoon

Tbsp = tablespoon

c = cup

oz = ounce

pt = pint

qt = quart

gal = gallon

lb = pound

= pound

g = gram

fl oz = fluid ounce

ABOUT THE AUTHOR

Josh Norris

Kimberly Danger is the founder and creator of Mommysavers.com and the family savings expert for Coupons.com, as well as a spokesperson for Uniroyal Tires. She is the author of *The Complete Book of Baby Bargains.* She lives in southern Minnesota with her husband and two kids.